WOMEN'S ROLES IN TECHNICAL INNOVATION

Food Cycle Technology Source Books

WOMEN'S ROLES IN TECHNICAL INNOVATION

IPEK ILKKARACAN and HELEN APPLETON

Practical
ACTION
PUBLISHING

Practical Action Publishing Ltd
27a Albert Street, Rugby, CV21 2SG, Warwickshire, UK
www.practicalactionpublishing.org

© The United Nations Development Fund for Women (UNIFEM), 1994, 1995
First published as *Women's Roles in the Innovation of Food Cycle Technologies* by
UNIFEM in 1994

First published 1995\ Digitised 2008

ISBN 10: 1 85339 307 X
ISBN 13: 9781853393075
ISBN Library Ebook: 9781780444475
Book DOI: http://dx.doi.org/10.3362/9781780444475

A catalogue record for this book is available from the British Library.

The authors, contributors and/or editors have asserted their rights under the
Copyright Designs and Patents Act 1988 to be identified as authors of their
respective contributions.

Since 1974, Practical Action Publishing has published and disseminated books
and information in support of international development work throughout
the world. Practical Action Publishing is a trading name of Practical Action
Publishing Ltd (Company Reg. No. 1159018), the wholly owned publishing
company of Practical Action. Practical Action Publishing trades only in support
of its parent charity objectives and any profits are covenanted back to Practical
Action (Charity Reg. No. 247257, Group VAT Registration No. 880 9924 76).

Illustrations by Matthew Whitton, UK, unless otherwise credited
Typeset by Dorwyn Ltd, Rowlands Castle, Hants, UK

Contents

Preface

This source book is one of a continuing UNIFEM series which aims to increase aware-ness of the range of technological options and sources of expertise, as well as indicating the complex nature of designing and successfully implementing technology develop-ment and dissemination programmes. While the other titles in the series concentrate on specific technical areas of the food cycle, this particular book explores the wealth of knowledge and skills that grassroots women possess in a variety of technical areas, and highlights the value of consulting them and adding to their own experience.

UNIFEM was established in 1976, and is an autonomous body associated since 1984 with the United Nations Development Programme. UNIFEM seeks to free women from under-productive tasks and augment the productivity of their work as a means of accelerating the development process. It does this through funding specific women's projects which yield direct benefits and through actions directed to ensure that all development policies, plans, programmes and projects take account of the needs of women producers.

In recognition of women's special roles in the production, processing, storage, pre-paration and marketing of food, UNIFEM initiated a Food Cycle Technology project in 1985 with the aim of promoting the widespread diffusion of tested technologies to increase the productivity of women's labour in this sector. While global in perspective, the initial phase of the project was implemented in Africa in view of the concern over food security in many countries of the region.

A careful evaluation of the African experience in the final phase of this five-year programme showed that there was a need for catalytic interventions which would lead to an enabling environment in which women would have easier access to technologies. This would be an environment where women producers could obtain information on the available technologies, have the capacity to analyse such information and make tech-nological choices on their own, as well as the capacity to acquire credit and training to enable the purchase and operation of the technology of their choice. This UNIFEM source book series aims to facilitate the building of such an environment.

Acknowledgements

This series of food cycle technology source books has been prepared at Intermediate Technology (IT) in the United Kingdom within the context of UNIFEM's Women and Food Cycle Technologies specialization.

During the preparation process the project staff contacted numerous project directors, rural development agencies, technology centres, women's organizations, equipment manufacturers and researchers in all parts of the world. The preparation of this particular volume has been based largely on the findings of a participatory research programme entitled *Do It Herself: Women and Technological Innovation*, and also draws on a wide range of literature and personal contacts.

The authors wish to thank the many agencies and individuals who have contributed to the preparation of this source book. Special thanks are owed to Marilyn Carr of UNIFEM who provided guidance to the research, devoted many hours to reading the drafts, correcting mistakes and suggesting how it could be improved, and the researchers of the *Do It Herself* (DIH) Programme, namely Hamid Dirar of Sudan, Josephine Mutagaywa and Winnie Ogana of Kenya, Erioth Simwogerere and Irene Wekiya of Uganda, Yvonne Wallace-Bruce of Ghana, Bernadette Lahai of Sierra Leone, Rodger Mpande and Noma Mpofu of Zimbabwe, Padmini Abeywardane and Kamala Peiris of Sri Lanka for their invaluable contribution to the research.

The authors would also like to thank UNIFEM and IT staff, particularly Mariama Djibo and Dagmar Schumacher of UNIFEM Tanzania and Ecuador offices, Mike Battcock of IT UK, Shaheda Azami, Priyanthi Fernando and Vishaka Hidalge of IT Bangladesh and Sri Lanka offices for their contributions to the Asia, Africa and Latin America case study material, Ilse Marks of UNIFEM New York for her technical editing, as well as Rose Delageot-Loial of UNIFEM New York, and Alison Gordon and Jill Georgiou of IT for their administrative support.

We are grateful to the following members of the editorial panel: Peg Snyder, the founding director of UNIFEM, Eremina Arishati Mvura and Rodger Mpande of the Ministry of Community Development and Ministry of Agriculture respectively in Zimbabwe, Kate Young of Womankind UK, and Kate Potts, then of IT, for their invaluable editorial comments.

The preparation of the source books was funded by UNIFEM with a cost-sharing contribution from the Government of Italy and the Government of the Netherlands. UNIFEM is also grateful to the Government of Italy, via the Italian Association of Women in Development (AIDOS), for sponsoring the translation of this series into French and Portuguese, and the printing of the first editions.

Ipek Ilkkaracan
UNIFEM

Helen Appleton
IT

Introduction

THIS SOURCE BOOK is one of the titles in the UNIFEM series on Women and Food Cycle Technologies. Unlike the other books, which have been designed to provide non-technical personnel involved in women's projects with preliminary technical information on specific areas of the food cycle, this volume aims to explain the importance of seeking out, starting with and adding to women's own technical knowledge and expertise.

Millions of people around the world, the majority of them women, manage to produce, process and market food with no external assistance, collectively utilizing thousands of years of experience and trial-and-error problem-solving methods, in order to meet the difficulties and opportunities presented by their local environments. Women's indigenous technical knowledge and innovative solutions to problems are in evidence across the whole range of food cycle activities. This book highlights the broad scope of expertise that exists in rural areas.

The book questions the low status accorded to women's technical knowledge, and challenges the assumption that it is inferior and non-scientific. It proposes a redefinition of 'science and technology', to include not only systematic research and development carried out in formal institutions, but also the generation of knowledge and skills through informal trial-and-error processes at the grassroots level.

The basic message to readers is that in the process of developing technologies, women, as users and producers, need to be consulted first, because they are the real 'experts'. Appropriate technical assistance builds on this expertise: technology institutions and local technical centres in all countries could and should be supporting women's own efforts to find solutions to technical problems. (See Appendix I for a list of contacts.)

The intended users of the book are the whole range of development practitioners who every day deal with issues of technology choice and diffusion within poverty alleviation programmes. When used as a companion to other books in the series, this book should greatly improve the environment within which technology projects are planned and implemented.

The source book is divided into five chapters. Chapter 1 gives a brief account of women's indigenous technical knowledge and its extent. Chapter 2 explores women's role in the innovation process and how technical assistance has conventionally ignored this.

The points made in these initial sections are illustrated and supported by the case studies in Chapter 3. Section I contains a number of case studies which illustrate the wealth of women's local technical knowledge and skills in food production and processing. The case studies in Section II indicate clearly that women are not merely passive owners of knowledge, but adapt and improve their traditional techniques in response to changing conditions. In Section III there are studies which illustrate how women can play an indirect yet important role in the development of equipment and techniques, in collaboration with development practitioners or local artisans.

The lessons which can be learned from the various case studies, and other literature reviewed, are presented in

Chapter 4. Chapter 5 draws on these lessons to offer guidelines for development practitioners working with women.

A list of organizations and initiatives which advocate the recognition of grassroots women's technological knowledge and skills, and promote participatory approaches to technology development based upon this local capacity is included in Appendix I. The publications and papers used in the preparation of the book are listed in Appendix II.

1
Local technological knowledge

Keepers of knowledge

WOMEN AND MEN have been involved in the gathering, production, processing and/or preparation of food for thousands of years, in an effort to meet their most basic need. In doing so, they have had to draw upon their knowledge of the surrounding environment. They have had to organize this knowledge in a particular way: hunt, gather wild plants, collect seeds, farm, carry out technical processes in converting these raw foods into an edible form and produce the tools and equipment necessary to make these tasks more efficient. All these activities are performed under a certain set of conditions, usually involving the climatic and agro-ecological characteristics of the area, the availability of material resources or energy and the level of labour skills and market demands (Warren *et al.*, 1989).

If food technology is seen as the knowledge and skills needed to produce and prepare the food necessary for survival, then peole have been generating and using food technologies ever since the very beginning of human existence. Based on centuries of experience, there exists a wealth of indigenous knowledge of food technology at local, grassroots level.

Examples of rural people utilizing their local knowledge in food production, processing and marketing are many. A few examples from around the world are:

o Bwa and Mossi cultivators of Burkina Faso use the leaves of the 'neem' tree (*Azadiarachta indica*) as an organic pesticide, mixing them with the stored cereal in their granaries to keep out insects (McCorkle, 1987).

o Groups in the Philippines intercrop pineapple, papaya, banana, and coconut in a single, small multi-storey plot. These producers can precisely explain and implement their complex, vertical cropping system in terms of a delicate balance between sunlight and shade, (Compton, 1989).

o In South America, the Quechua Indians' diagnosis of contagious livestock diseases in their sheep, which is based partly on 16th century Iberian notions of 'hot and cold diseases' and partly on Incaic concepts of 'evil winds', is accurate and their curative techniques are effective (McCorkle, 1987).

Low status of people's knowledge

Only in the last 200 years has empirical knowledge been joined by a radically new kind of knowledge – 'scientific' knowledge gained through the procedures of research (Maybury, 1982). It is because of the recent development of science and technology as an institutional practice that the thousands of years of indigenous knowledge, scientific understanding and people's technology have become invisible.

Indigenous knowledge, as it is transferred from one generation to another in the form of beliefs and common practices, is often undermined by scientists as being of little value in comparison to formal scientific knowledge. Local people have been repeatedly told that the knowledge and way of doing things common in their culture are inferior, and that their practices are not 'scientific'. As the case studies in this book will show, however, there are many cases where local technologies prove to be better than the ones suggested by the professionals, and grassroots people's knowledge is often more extensive regarding their surrounding environment and immediate needs.

In Kenya, many irrigation schemes constructed to fit a 'scientific' model have failed. 'Even irrigation administrators admit that such systems are unable to better, or even match, the performance of centuries old, small-scale irrigation techniques used by local peoples like the Taita,' and throughout Africa, the traditional technique of intercropping has been proven to give much better yields than the monocropping technique suggested by most 'expert' agronomists (McCorkle, 1989).

In Bali, Western-style irrigated, high-productivity agriculture based on the widespread use of chemicals as fertilizers and pesticides turned out to be more vulnerable to viral and bacterial diseases and plagues of rodents and insects. These new methods also poisoned the water and the soil and killed the fish upon which people depended for their protein and ultimately depressed crop yields (Cowley 1989, Lansing 1987 in McCorkle, 1989).

The 'Citemene' system in Zambia, the traditional technique for maintaining soil fertility, also illustrates a local technology that is more 'ecologically sound'. For many years, the farmers of Zambia logged trees, burned branches and used ash as a fertilizer for the soil. Owing to the nature of the tropical soil, which is very fragile and requires a variety of agricultural techniques, the Citemene worked well in Zambia. Land could be used for five years before being left to rest. Under colonial rule, however, the white settlers, who promoted exhaustive use of the land, dismissed the Citemene as backward and destructive, without any effort to find out why the local farmers used this particular conservation method. Instead continuous monocropping was promoted, which exhausted the soil to the extent that in some regions of the country, such as Kabwe, farms have been abandoned and workers have migrated to urban centres, where they can barely survive. Consequently Zambia, where food riots are now common, has joined the long list of African food aid recipients (Katumba, 1991).

The Machakos area in central Kenya, where the introduction of modern agricultural techniques has aggravated the consequences of a lack of rainfall, is another area where the local producers are trying to return to traditional methods of cultivation. Previously, food was intercropped in this area – sorghum and millet were grown in rows, with other crops in between. Both were left standing after harvest to prevent soil erosion by wind and water, and leaves from the crops were left on the ground as a mulch, which prevented water loss by evaporation. Cow dung was used as fertilizer. This order was disrupted under the colonial administration, which saw the traditional intercropped gardens as a confused mess. The outsiders, failing to take into account the fragility of marginal lands, imposed practices such as monocropping, clearing great tracts of land and ploughing for cash crop cultivation at the expense of indigenous crops and subsistence farming, which in turn called for the use of chemical fertilizers to maintain declining productivity. Over the years, these externally introduced techniques have proved to be ecologically disastrous. Soil erosion has intensified, gradually limiting crop yields and reducing grazing pastures. Rapid population and livestock growth has further aggravated the effects, causing local producers to revert to the traditional techniques which had worked for previous generations (Ogana, undated).

It is important to acknowledge that neither local knowledge nor 'Western' or 'institutional scientific' knowledge are perfect in all aspects. Local methods of trial and error do not always achieve the level of precision that the controlled environment of a scientific laboratory affords. On the other hand, the isolation of institutional R&D from the real conditions of production can lead to innovations with little or no practical application. Institutional science and technology does have something to offer to grassroots knowledge, but technical change is most successful when it is based on the knowledge and skills of local people, and is under their full control.

When 'people' are 'women'

Given that, all over the world, providing food is regarded as a woman's job, it can be said that when it comes to food 'people' are 'women'; that is, most of the indigenous knowledge about food is owned by women. This technical knowledge enables women to continue to feed the population despite deteriorating agro-ecological conditions and their lack of access to improved technologies. In Nigeria, for instance, women food producers use natural fertilizers and pesticides as effective and low-cost control measures. The traditional pesticides, which are non-toxic and biodegradable, come from Nigeria's diverse flora, such as pepper fruit (*Dennettia tripetela*), a shrub that bears spicy fruits with a distinctive fragrance, and *Piper guineense*, a pungent variety of brown pepper that has been found useful in traditional medical practices. These local techniques sustain women's production, and are ecologically more sound

than modern fertilizers and pesticides (Spurling, 1991; Ononiwu, 1991).

The lack of understanding of indigenous technological knowledge and practices is accentuated where women are involved. In many countries, productive activities and responsibilities are clearly divided between men and women, and women are usually in charge of all household food production, processing and marketing. Often men have little or no understanding of women's activities, and do not share women's knowledge. Even when technology development activities are designed around indigenous knowledge, they can fail due to the false identification of who holds which information in a community. For example, a research programme co-ordinated by the University of Missouri and aimed at the exploration of local knowledge of livestock diseases in the Peruvian peasant communities addressed itself to the male heads of household. Men, however, showed more interest in projects on plant crops, and displayed little knowledge about problems of livestock in their villages. When the researchers realized that women are responsible for the herding, and began to involve women, the true extent of local livestock knowledge was revealed (Fernandez 1986 in McCorkle, 1989).

Why have women been ignored?

Women's indigenous technical knowledge can and should form a solid basis for technology development activities, and yet it continues to be ignored by people working in these areas. One reason for this is that much of what women do is labelled 'domestic', which means that their activities are probably of lower status and less visible to the casual (male) observer. A second reason is that very few women are involved in extension services, or in decision making, technical development or formal research. Men working in these areas simply do not meet and talk to women during the working day. Neither are they challenged about the assumptions which they make about the nature of productive roles and responsibilities. A 1987 study conducted in Kenya, Malawi, Sierra Leone, Zambia and Zimbabwe reveals the common images of women held by men involved in agricultural extension work.

o Women do not make significant contributions to agriculture.
o Women are always tied down with household chores and children.
o Women are shy and difficult to reach.
o Women are difficult to gather in one place, even if their interests converge.
o Women are unprogressive in dealing with innovations. (Gill quoted in Awa, 1989)

The fact that technical and development specialists, both expatriate and national, have little understanding of women's contributions to household survival means that the decisions that they make and have made about development priorities in a particular region have been based on assumptions which undermine women's roles and technical capacities. It also means that technical experts do not even think of consulting women, and information about new technologies is given to men in rural areas even when men are in no position to use their new knowledge.

Despite the fact that women probably form the majority of small-scale technology users, they are rendered economically and technologically insignificant.

A further factor that undermines

women's technological capabilities is the assumption that technology is 'neutral'. This assumption ignores the social and cultural priorities that shape the development of any technology, and overlooks the gender-specific nature of food production, where women's needs are different from those of men. For example, the increasing use of the custom rice-mill in Bangladesh – logical from a narrow economic perspective of productivity – deprives the poor women, who previously earned money by milling rice for richer families, of a livelihood. The effects of this technology have not been 'neutral' or 'gender-neutral'. The few jobs created by the use of the custom mill have gone to men (Whitehead in Ahmed, 1985).

The technological invisibility of women has been supported by lack of acknowledgement, both at national and international levels, of women's economic contribution. National and international statistics, which form the basis for resource allocation and major policy decisions, do not estimate the value of so-called 'unpaid' work. This means that most subsistence activities, on which rural people's lives depend, are not reflected in development plans and priorities. Policies tend to favour large-scale production over small-scale, and will detract from the importance of women's knowledge and use of technology. The problem is further compounded by the fact that development plans usually treat the rural household as a single economic unit, where the interests of all household members are perceived to be the same as those of the 'head of household', who is assumed to be a man. This despite the fact that responsibilities for different aspects of household production may be quite separate, and in some countries up to 50 per cent of households may be female-headed as a result of male migration.

2
Technological change and innovation by women

WHILE THE understanding of women's roles in utilizing, preserving and transferring indigenous technological knowledge is very limited, an understanding of their role in the technological innovation process is almost non-existent. Even those who admit that women know a great deal about the soils, trees and crops upon which their families depend, are less willing to accept that women are also actively involved in adapting their tools and techniques to changing circumstances.

What is innovation?

Part of the problem is defining what is meant by innovation. Technological innovation is usually carried out by men in technology research and development institutions. Traditionally it has focused on the design of hardware – equipment or machinery – and has implied the development of a new product.

However, technology innovation is not only the design of a clever piece of machinery or a technique. It is also the process through which improved machinery or techniques become an integral part of the whole production system, suitably adapted to the users and their environments. As the following case studies will show, all over the world, women constantly modify, adapt or change production processes in response to certain problems, such as national disasters, environmental changes, market demands, conflicts and many more. However small these changes may be they are also innovations: they illustrate a process of problem identification and solving similar to

that carried out in technical research establishments. If technical assistance is to succeed in enabling some of the poorest peoples to improve the quality of their lives, technical specialists must recognize and build on the expertise of those with the most comprehensive local knowledge.

Why has external innovation failed?

A research and development specialist designing a technology in the North, makes assumptions about users and environments based on his or her own knowledge of Northern societies. Clearly, the experience of a person living in Europe or North America is completely different from that of a rural African, Asian or Latin American woman. He or she may have a wide knowledge about different types of equipment, materials and chemical processes, but is less aware of the mechanisms by which people adapt technologies to their own use, and of the circumstances which define their priorities. Even within the same country, differences of class, race, ethnicity, religion and gender can render the experiences of technical experts living in urban areas completely different from those of poor rural women. Many experts have not considered that they may have something to learn from women's technical knowledge and skills. To cite an example encountered recently, a technologist commenting on a paper about women's innovation in Asia, said 'I've never heard of this technique before. It must just be some old crone in the hills'. Other food technologists, asked to comment on the same paper, replied that the innovation was widespread and practised by many women in the area.

Hence, technical assistance has traditionally been based on technical design and innovation being carried out by people, often outsiders, who do not understand how a rural community's priorities are shaped, the value of women's productive roles, or the important contributions that women themselves can make. Most technical improvements thus obtained have then been 'transferred' to the users for testing. Users, especially if they happen to be women, in many cases have been perceived as passive recipients, and their knowledge and their priorities have not been considered. These 'transferred' improvements have also often depended on purchased materials, which for poor producers has tended to introduce problems of reliable access to credit and the supply of materials and spare parts.

The irrigated rice development project in the Gambia is one such example of the failure of technology transfer. The project set out to introduce new techniques of rice cultivation under irrigation, using high-yielding varieties, fertilizers and some mechanization. The project was designed around working with men, although women were the ones traditionally responsible for rice production in this area. The men were offered capital equipment, advice from extension workers on credit and other inputs in order to expand their production. One of the main bottlenecks they faced was the shortage of labour, particularly during the rainy season when women had their own fields to cultivate, combined with the inaccessibility of traditionally female skills in transplanting and weeding. The women had no obligation to work for the men since the income generated through male-controlled production was not guaranteed to benefit the family in general. Men were neither able to perform all of the work for expanded production by themselves, nor did they have the money to hire female labour. The planners' ignorance of the existing gender roles in production, among other factors, led to the failure of the project (Dey, 1981).

Research by experts and subsequent transfer of technology are further complicated by the need of poorer small-scale producers to diversify production. The majority of small-scale producers, particularly in the tropical south, are women, working with limited resources. The production systems in which they are involved are often complex and diverse in order to spread risks. Spreading of risks is crucial to survival in areas where production is erratic or seasonal, harvests unreliable and prices beyond the control of the local market. Simple transfer of standard technology packages, however, usually encourages specialization and thereby increases vulnerability to disasters by decreasing people's capacity to diversify.

The prevailing framework of most technology development programmes has been set by variations of a technology transfer approach, although occasionally some sort of consultation may have been carried out. In some cases, technologists have consulted with small-scale producers about local needs and priorities, and have even developed the technology on site, but local people were still seen in a passive 'user' role. Even technical programmes that have been set up with a view to enabling local producers to participate in technology development in a more active way have tended to founder, because the priorities, knowledge and control have continued to remain the property of the outsiders. Small producers have not been able to break free of this relationship of dependence.

The technology development approach promoted throughout this source book is one that fully integrates people's local, grassroots technical knowledge and supports people themselves as the innovators and the owners of the process. Although some understanding of people's indigenous technical knowledge and innovation has been developed over the years, it has not yet become an integral part of thinking about technology development.

While there are some examples of participatory technology development, programmes to support technological innovations directly by small producers themselves are very few indeed. Most science and technology development efforts lack any recognition of the local capacity to innovate in general, and in particular of women's contributions to innovation and technical change.

Why are outsiders needed?

If women are capable of instigating technical change on their own, then why is there a need for external intervention at all? Although women innovate all the time, and will continue to do so, the process is not perfect. Women are constrained by lack of time, lack of credit and lack of information about raw materials, improved technologies and markets. Development organizations should be working with women to identify such constraints and help them use their own technical skills and innovative capacities to improve production. Appropriate technical assistance is not always a new machine. It may involve supporting local innovation by arranging links with other women, or by arranging for women to participate in literacy training. Whatever the support required it is essential that women themselves remain in control of the initiative.

Recent attempts to support innovation by women

There have been some attempts at the macro-level to recognize and support innovation by women. A few recent research efforts have attempted to rectify the gender imbalance of innovation policies, through promoting an awareness of the existence of women inventors around the world. *Women Inventors*, a book by Farag Moussa from the World Intellectual Property Organisation (WIPO) and the President of the International Federation of Inventors Associations (IFIA), is one of the few attempts to prove that women are equally capable of technological innovation, that they can be as creative as men, and that the world of technical change is not a male preserve. The book illustrates the scope and range of women's technological innovations, and provides profiles of contemporary women inventors, from 26 countries on three continents. The oldest woman is 81, while the youngest is only six. Their discoveries and innovations range from the very simple to the very sophisticated, such as an eye-surgery technique which won the Nobel Prize. Other examples include computers for autistic children, a new breed of cattle, safe switches, ultra-thin photographs and a knitting machine.

Magdelena Villacruz from the Philippines is one of the role models in this book. Named the 'inventor of the year' in the Philippines in 1986, she has 15 patented inventions to her credit – all in the 'unfeminine' field of agricultural mechanics. The most successful invention, and Ms Villacruz's main stock-in-trade, is a tractor especially designed for use in wet soil.

Through the presentation of such a broad spectrum of personalities and fields of activity, the message conveyed is that creative ideas are not a prerogative of men — women can grasp technology, they can master its complexities, and even construct life-saving devices.

The Women Inventors and Scientists Workshop, which was organized by the Women Inventors Association of the Philippines (WIAPI) and the Women Scientists Forum of Thailand in Bangkok in August 1991, was another attempt to provide the opportunity to share women's technological innovations and research and development efforts in both countries. The technological innovations discussed at the workshop ranged from home-based to industrial production. From Thailand, women's innovation of commercial production technologies for mushroom cultivation and industrial fish-sauce fermentation were described. In the Philippines, methods of solar and mechanical drying of tropical fruits and the ideal processing conditions were identified, as well as improved recipes for longer shelf-life tamarind juice concentrate and candies, and various technologies for coconut processing for cream, milk, skimmed milk, water and meal production. Some of the technologies discussed at the workshop, such as improved production and processing of seaweed value-added products in Thailand, are in the pilot-testing phase.

Grassroots women also innovate

While efforts like this workshop fulfil an important role in the promoting and recognition of professional women's contribution to the formal Research and Development efforts, it is crucial, at the same time, to challenge the failure of technical innovation and development policies to understand and build on local, grassroots capacity to innovate and instigate technical change. Many women's innovations, which occur in domestic activities or in the informal context of village production, are not 'owned' by anyone and as such remain unacknowledged. As a consequence, the potential for improving livelihoods remains unrecognized and untapped.

The case studies in the following sections illustrate how grassroots women constantly modify their activities of food production, processing and marketing in response to changes in their environment, availability of resources (such as time, labour, raw products, fuelwood, water), market demands and other factors. They show that women do not passively watch the conditions of production, such as the fuelwood crisis, worsen around them. On the contrary they do whatever they can to find their own solutions to the problems afflicting them.

3
Case studies

THE CASE STUDIES in this section are grouped into three parts, showing the different roles that women play in technological change. The case studies in Section I explore the extent and nature of women's indigenous technological knowledge. These examples illustrate not only that rural women's indigenous knowledge of food production, processing and marketing is much more complicated and technically profound than is generally assumed, but also that this knowledge plays a vital role in the survival and well-being of families and communities.

The case studies in Section II are about technological innovation and change instigated by women on their own, and show that women's local knowledge is not static. They illustrate women's capacity to use their technical expertise and skills in order to change, adapt and innovate food production, processing and marketing techniques, and also the factors that encourage and support women's innovative thinking. Examples are wideranging. In some cases, what may seem like a simple innovation has been shown to have a vital impact: for example, women's discovery of new sources of food among the wild plants and trees in Zimbabwe has improved food security in an agriculturally infertile area. In other cases, the innovation involves significant changes in techniques of production and design of processing equipment as illustrated by the case study of women salt producers in Sierra Leone.

The case studies in Section III are examples of women's innovation with external support. They illustrate some of the many ways that external intervention can and should facilitate local capacity to innovate and generate technologies, and how intermediary agencies or development practitioners can provide their services to grassroots women in strengthening informal research and development activities.

All case studies in this section were compiled by the authors from original material referenced at the end of each case study.

Section I
Women's local knowledge

Fermented foods in Sudan

Sudanese women possess a deep scientific knowledge and understanding of the sophisticated processes which they use in food fermentation.

Sudan has about 60 different kinds of fermented food products prepared from a myriad of substrates. Of these, about 30 are made from sorghum or millet, grains which have been an important part of Sudan's food culture for thousands of years.

The most complicated sorghum fermentation process that the women carry out is

Figure 1. An ancient rock carving found at Jebel Qeili in the southern Butana shows a goddess presenting King Sherkarer with sorghum for his victory

the preparation of a clear sorghum beer called *assaliya*. The 40-step process produces a malt syrup from germinated sorghum grain and takes two days or more to complete (see Figure 3).

Among the most common sorghum foods in Sudan are a fermented stiff porridge called *aceda*, a fermented bread called *kissra*, and a drink called *abreh*. While women's preparation of each product entails a complicated process, given the limitation of space, we will describe only the fermentation of *abreh* here. The process is also outlined in Figure 4.

The processing technique of *abreh*

Sudanese women prepare *abreh*, a traditional and popular non-alcoholic fermented sorghum drink, usually for the holy month of Ramadan. *Abreh* is in the form of fine flakes which are added to cold water, sweetened to taste and then swallowed whole while drinking.

The grains are first washed and dehulled using a wooden mortar and pestle. The peeled grains are then washed again. Then the grains are wet milled on the *murhaka* (traditional milling stone) to give *derish* which is allowed to ferment. After 24 hours of fermentation, wet milling continues for one to three days until a very fine paste is obtained. When all the *abreh ajin* (dough) has been wet milled, part of it is cooked into a thin porridge and the porridge is left to cool for a further 24 hours before being returned to the remaining *ajin* bulk with some spices, such as black cumin (*Negila sativa*).

The second stage of fermentation continues for about three to six days until the

A. SORGHUM MALT PRODUCTS

I. Non-alcoholic products

1. *Breads*

    i. Huhi-mur
    ii. Kissra-assala

2. *Dumplings, granules and meal*

    i. Hussuwa
    ii. Um Narein
    iii. Um Shappa
    iv. Soorji Ramadam
    v. Khemiss Tweira

II. Alcoholic products

    i. Merissa
    ii. Assaliya
    iii. Baganiya

B. SORGHUM GRAIN PRODUCTS

I. Porridges

1. *Thick porridges*

    i. Aceda*
    ii. Otam*
    iii. Dibliba*
    iv. Damirga*
    v. Jiriya*

2. *Thin porridges*

    i. Nasha*
    ii. Madida*
    iii. Raghida*
    iv. Agoud*

3. *Thick brittle discs*

    i. Gurrassah*
    ii. Hadeeb*
    iii. Tukkab*
    iv. Khulassa*

4. *Granules*

    i. Mongakebo*
    ii. Busseib*

II. Breads

1. *Extra-thin sheets*

    i. Kissra*
    ii. Abreh*

2. *Thin sheets*

    i. Kissrat-kass*
    ii. Kissrat-ker**
    iii. Kissra-murra**
    iv. Um-kushuk*

* Products from standard *ajin*
** Products from special *ajins*.

Figure 2. Classification of Sudan's fermented sorghum products

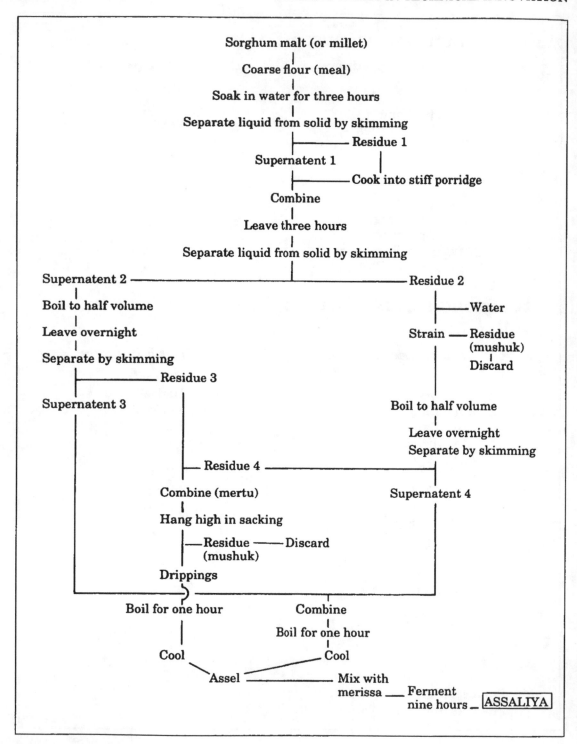

Figure 3. *Assaliya* production

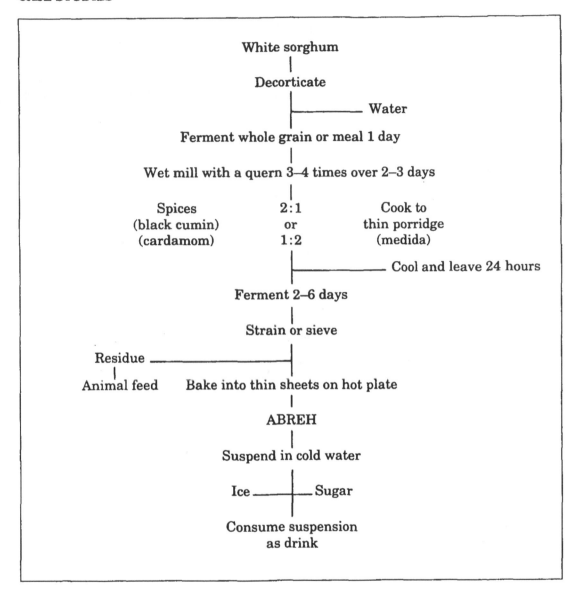

Figure 4. *Abreh* production process

stiff dough becomes liquid. About 50ml of the dough is poured into a *doka* (ceramic pan), covering the whole surface. The dough is spread flat and thin, baked, and swept into a container. Because the sheet is very thin it breaks into flakes when it is swept off the hot plate.

The advantages of *abreh* and other fermented foods

The *abreh* drink, which has a fresh sour taste, fulfils the role of a nutritious thirst-quencher in the hot climate of Sudan. The Sudanese believe that a drink of *abreh* is a healthier way of satisfying thirst than plain water. In addition to being nutritious, the acidity of fermented sorghum decreases the risks involved in using contaminated water. Moreover, the flakes are lightweight and easily transportable for travellers. Fermentation is a valuable method of preserving food for times of scarcity, and *abreh*, like other fermented food products, can be stored for a long time. Fermentation also improves the digestibility of a food, enabling women to produce high value additions to the diet from substances such as bones, leaves, caterpillars and cow urine. In the Sudanese context, women's knowledge of fermented foodstuffs has played an important role in coping with periods of famine, but a lack of understanding of these skills has led to international aid agencies organizing relief operations around imported foodstuffs.

When mechanization takes over . . .
(based on interview with A.W. Musa)

Abdul Wahab Musa's *kissra* and *abreh* factory in Khartoum is one of the first examples of the mechanized processing of traditional foods in Sudan. The roller drier machine that Musa has designed can produce a variety of sorghum products simply by adjusting the speed of the conveyor belt and the temperature of the heating system under it.

In order to develop this machine, Musa consulted closely with women producers of sorghum foods. 'Women are the ones who have been processing sorghum to make these traditional foods for hundreds of years in Sudan, and are therefore the experts. Their feedback and inputs were crucial.'

While Musa's machine has the potential for relieving Sudanese women from a laborious task that they have been performing for years, it also carries the threat of pushing the many rural and peri-urban women producers and marketers of fermented sorghum products out of the market. The factory-produced foods are sold directly to urban consumers for lower prices. Some people, however, still prefer to buy sorghum products from women producers, who make them using traditional technology, since the taste of the factory products has not achieved the traditional standards. Nevertheless, the price difference of 5 Sudanese pounds (approx. US$ 0.6) per sheet of *kissra* bread has serious implications for women's production.

Having first proved the capacity of his machine, Musa applied to two famine relief agencies for support in disseminating the product. He reasons that women's sorghum production and processing activities have been crucial in the survival of rural communities and that upgrading of local techniques can further improve the existing capacity for food security. One of the agencies was initially interested, but no conclusion was reached owing to disagreement over the price of the machine. The other agency wrote back saying they were not interested. (Dirar, 1991)

Moringa oleifera seeds as natural water coagulants, Sudan

This case study illustrates that women's techniques for water purification parallel those of water treatment plants.

Eighty per cent of the population of Sudan live in the rural areas where water is of vital importance, both with respect to availability and quality. Women have to use muddy water from the rivers or intermittent streams (*khours*) during the rainy season or turbid water from natural rain

***Kissra* producer in Khartoum using the traditional method**

***Kissra* production on the mechanized roller and drier designed by a Sudanese engineer**

The factory-produced sorghum products: *kissra* bread (front right), packaged *abreh* (back right), and a Sudanese adaptation of corn flakes using sorghum (left)

ponds and from artificial rain catchments (*hafirs*) during most of the year.

Women traditionally treat the drinking and cooking water, which they bring in twice daily, in the morning and before sunset, using natural coagulants of plant and soil origin and in some areas using alum and soda. The latter method, although used as an essential water coagulant in public water works, is less favoured by women, since drinking water treated with alum is believed to cause gastro-intestinal disturbances and also result in abortions. Hence, rural women prefer to limit the use of alum to washing water only, and use moringa seeds for drinking water. Indeed, laboratory tests show that moringa seeds compare favourably to alum and other commonly used water coagulants with respect to the rate of reaction and the decrease in the turbidity of the treated water (alum achieves only 1 per cent higher purification than moringa seeds).

The traditional method is to crush the seeds in mortars and then add the powder to a small amount of water in a deep plate or a calabash, and sometimes stir for 10–30 minutes. The suspension is then poured into turbid water in a water jar of burnt clay or other material. Some women in the Blue Nile Province place the crushed seeds in a small bag of thin cloth to which a thread is attached and stir the bag in turbid water in the jars in order to effectively clarify the water with a filtered extract of seeds. The seeds cause the impurities in the water to clot and then the water is filtered or left to settle down before drinking.

Rural women claim that the wings of the seeds should be removed before crushing in the mortar, but that the seed coat should be left or only partially removed for best results. Laboratory experiments, which compared whole seed powder with powder of seed pulp, have proved this claim to be accurate. The seed coats are removed only in cases where they are used as folk medicine.

Other traditional uses of moringa seeds

In addition to their traditional use as water coagulants, *Moringa oleifera* seeds are also used as food and folk medicine in Sudan, as well as in other parts of Africa and Asia. In Tanzania they are added to curries, and in India they are fried, tasting like peanuts. In Sudan and Northern Nigeria they are used as a hot tea treatment for gastro-intestinal troubles. In Egypt they are replaced for the same purpose by *Moringa peregrina* seeds. In India and Pakistan they are used in addition as antipyretic (preventing or alleviating fever), purgative, and against enlargement of the liver and spleen.

Indigenous knowledge of natural coagulants in other countries

Water purification with natural coagulants of plant origin is not only carried out in Sudan, but also in rural areas of other countries. Women in India have used *nirmali* seeds for centuries to clarify muddy waters when the mud in Indian rivers increases during the monsoon. In the villages the nirmali seeds are ground on a rough stone and mixed to a paste with water which is then added to the raw water. In Peru, women traditionally use 'tuna', a cactus brought by Spanish invaders from Mexico. The cactus leaves are broken, the sap is allowed to trickle out and is then stirred into the turbid water. In Northern Chad and Northern Nigeria, women use plant ash of any origin as a water coagulant. (Jahn and Dirar, 1979)

Fermented milk in Kenya

Kenyan women's scientific knowledge and skills in milk processing contribute significantly to food security.

For many rural women in Kenya, the treatment and storage of milk before consumption is a traditional skill. Dairy researchers in the country have recently started taking an interest in the processes that pastoral women use in the processing of milk.

With livestock being the mainstay of most pastoralist families, milk is usually the most readily available food for the children. Traditionally, the Kalenjin, a linguistic cluster of seven tribes, must have at least one cow in each homestead. Where the family is too poor to afford one, community members (some of whom have up to two hundred head of cattle), lend them several cows, to be returned after calving. The poor family keeps the calves, and in that way begin their own herd. No herd means no food.

The treatment of milk

Pastoral women have different processing methods whose length and complexity depend on the nature of settlement. Nomadic pastoralists like the Masai and Samburu have shorter milk-processing procedures and shorter-lived products. Settled pastoralists like the Tugen, Kipsigis and Nandi have more elaborate processes which preserve the milk for relatively longer periods.

Different pastoral groups likewise use different methods to store the milk in gourds. In preparing the gourd, the Tugen women, for instance, make a brush from the stick of the *sosisondo* tree to clean the inside. Brushes made from this tree are tough and may last for up to two years before replacement. Samburu women use the curved mid-rib of the stalk of palm leaf. The curved end is chewed into a brush-like tool for use, and is ideal for cleaning out pumpkin-shaped gourds.

Leaves with a rough texture, used to dislodge the fat embedded in the inside walls of the gourd, have a scouring effect. An alternative to the leaves is a handful of small stones. The gourd is not considered clean until it has been washed out three or four times in warm or cold water. It is then ready for drying, in a shaded area, for at least a day.

Charcoal, formed from the smouldering embers of branches from the *ite* tree is used as a milk preservative. Women use the embers to coat the inside of the cleaned gourd. The charcoal has various effects. It lines the inside of the gourd, reducing its porosity and therefore making it airtight. The smoke from the embers also has a preservative effect which prevents bacterial multiplication that causes spoilage, while allowing simultaneous souring. The charcoal smoke imparts a special flavour to the milk, and a bluish colour which is of high aesthetic value to the consumer.

'Our men' says Gaslight, a young woman from the Tugen tribe, 'take milk only from the gourd. Milk from elsewhere is inferior. We believe all cattle in the world belong to us and that nobody knows more about milk that we do.'

Having prepared the gourd, women pasteurize the milk by boiling. The pasteurized milk is left to cool before being poured into the gourd to prevent the growth of spoiling micro-organisms. Mothers training their daughters in the treatment of milk emphasize that hot milk is never poured into a gourd. Finally the gourd is corked to render it airtight, making is possible for the milk to be preserved for up to a month.

Milk as a means of survival

Milk has a special significance for pastoral people, who treat it as an important element of food security for their families. The gourds are put in a *lengut* (wooden crate) in a corner to serve as a drink cabinet. Visitors are served milk from this cabinet, which in some houses may store up to 50 gourds.

On occasions such as weddings or circumcision ceremonies, milk is served abundantly as a refreshing drink. To symbolize the importance of milk to survival, brides are presented with gourds. A mixture of milk and blood constitutes the main diet of newly circumcised boys who stay in the bush for two to three months. The mixture of these two ingredients together is a popular nutritious drink not only for circumcised boys, but also for children in general and mothers who have given birth.

To prepare this drink, women use a forked stick to beat up the blood, drawn from a healthy animal, to remove fibrinogen which causes the blood to clot if present. The ratio of milk to blood is about 4:1, and it may be either consumed immediately, or boiled and stored for use after spontaneous fermentation. (Ogana, 1988)

Milk production and processing in Nigeria

This case study emphasizes the need for governments and development planners to understand women's local production systems.

Throughout northern and central Nigeria, as in many other parts of West Africa, dairy products suited to local tastes and conditions are sold daily at markets, on roadsides, and at house doors. While men manage and milk the cattle, it is exclusively the Fulani pastoral women who process and market dairy products in this area, based on traditional technologies. The herd manager decides on the level of milk production and its allocation to the women in the household, while women decide how much of the milk allocated to them is kept for the family and how much is sold.

Women hardly ever sell fresh whole milk. A few women sell fermented whole milk mixed with cooked cereal, and Hausa women sell a soft white cheese which is usually cut into squares and fried for selling in the wet season. The cheese is not stored but sold a few days after production. Fulani women normally make butter every second day. The skimmed milk left after butter making is stirred briskly into a liquid called *nono*. *Nono* is usually, and most profitably, sold mixed with sugar and a mashed grain called *fura*, and therefore most women regard *fura* making as an integral part of their dairy business. In the dry season *nono* is also combined with water and *kuka*, the acid pith of baobab fruits (*Adansonia digitata*). Rich in vitamin C, *kuka* is an important complement to milk and cereal foods, and without milk is also used as a traditional beverage in northern Nigeria.

Fermented milk is highly suitable for the local conditions of production and consumption. In areas where milk cannot easily be kept cool, marketing of fermented milk rather than fresh milk allows the women more flexibility in marketing with respect to time and distance. The fermentation process prevents the growth of disease-causing micro-organisms, rendering the product safer than fresh milk. During fermentation the lactose in the milk is converted into lactic acid which prevents the product from causing adverse effects in people with lactose intolerance.

The importance of marketing

The women usually spend four to five hours every other day selling their dairy products to regular customers in their neighbourhood and at various sites in town. They travel on foot, and carry their produce on their heads. The women who live closer to town prefer to sell in town, since they receive higher prices there than in the villages. Some Fulani women in richer, or strictly muslim households, however, do not retail the milk themselves but rather sell to middlewomen, who resell the milk at a higher price together with *fura*.

Despite the efficiency of women's indigenous milk processing and marketing techniques, dairy development efforts in Nigeria allocate considerable resources to the designing of high-technology plants to make conventional European milk products. One reason for the neglect of local dairy products and dairywomen in development planning, as well as for the poor record of smallholder dairy development, is the planners' lack of knowledge about traditional milk production, processing and marketing. Closer study of the activities of dairywomen in a Fulani settlement area in central Nigeria revealed that the main problems faced by the producers were not in processing and marketing but in milk production.

While the women are convinced that they could process and sell more milk if they had more, they do not receive enough milk from the family herds to be able to increase their production. Men tend to seek benefits through greater calf survival and herd growth by leaving more milk for the calves. Women claim that if they were to contribute toward herd inputs, they could not be sure that they would receive more milk as a direct result, since it is the men who decide how the inputs are used and who also control the

milking. The collection of milk for processing at the recently formed dairy plants is likely to divert from Fulani women's already scarce raw product and their access to cash income, and diminish the supply to traditional markets for low-income consumers. (Waters-Bayer, 1986)

Traditional food storage in Kenya

This case study illustrates the importance of building on low-cost local techniques for food storage.

As elsewhere in Africa, Kenya experiences post-harvest food crop losses of 30–40 per cent. This figure is quite significant in a country where only 17.5 per cent of the land is of high or medium agricultural potential, although agriculture is the backbone of the national economy. Some 80 per cent of Kenya's population, estimated at 23 million, live on this land, and the population is growing at 3.5 per cent annually. Most of the remaining land is arid or semi-arid, and is suitable only for nomadic pastoralism. It is under these circumstances that Kenyan women have to feed the nation.

Most Kenyan women (88 per cent) live in rural areas, where they are mainly occupied with agricultural and household chores. Women have traditionally contributed most of the labour required for subsistence farming, and also spend much of their labour on the production of cash crops.

'There was more food in the past when the soil was more fertile. Then you could dig a small area and get a good harvest, but now you have to dig a relatively large area to get the same yield, and that can be accomplished only by using a tractor, which is too expensive for most people', says Nyeyu, an old woman farmer of the Griama ethnic group, living in Kilifi District in Eastern Kenya. For Nyeyu it is now even more important to preserve whatever little she is able to harvest.

The *lutsaga*

A substantial portion of crop yield is wasted each year owing to lack of storage facilities as well as processing capacities. The foodstuffs are spoilt mainly by insects, rodents such as rats and mice, as well as moulds and fungi. Climatic conditions such as moisture and warm temperature encourage the growth of moulds and fungi, while inadequate storage structures promote spoilage.

Rural women, having limited income to purchase pesticides, have to rely on indigenous technology to store and preserve their produce. This indigenous storage technology, called the *lutsaga*, is a traditional granary built from rafters and sticks over the three-stone fire. The *lutsaga*, which is raised about 1.5m above the cooking area in the kitchen, has a roof that prevents attacks by birds and protects the stored food from adverse weather.

The smoke rising from the fire coats the seeds with a protective layer. The coating protects the seeds against spoilage, and crops stored in the *lutsaga* remain clean and freer than when they are laid bare on the ground to be sun-dried. Only when the insect population becomes too large are pesticides used. Rats are usually left for cats to take care of. When that fails, however, maize flour is mixed with pesticides to be used as a bait.

The *lutsaga*, although used mainly for grains like maize, cowpeas, rice and beans, could also serve to store fruits like bananas and mangoes, or tomatoes, which gradually ripen, warmed by heat from the fire below. Occasionally women

preserve *mkunde* leaves in the *lutsaga*, which dry to crispness and may be used as vegetables months later.

Apart from preventing the waste and spoilage of the stored produce, another advantage of the *lutsaga* is that it facilitates proper drying of the grains, making them easier to pound.

Therefore it is with regret that Nyeyu points out: 'Traditionally every Griama home had a *lutsaga*. But from the current trend it seems that future generations will not have a *lutsaga*. Having to go to school, they are not keen on farming. Somehow, they will have to figure out what to eat in the future. By then, we, the older generation, will be gone . . .'

Nyeyu's concern for the future generations' food security is shared by many others in Kenya who criticize the undermining of the need to teach children to value the land and its produce. Formal education has tended to stress the higher-paid, urban white collar jobs, which has caused the younger generation to look down on manual labour in rural areas. (Ogana, undated)

Fruit preservation in Sri Lanka

This case study emphasizes the understanding women have of the processes which they are using, and the importance of traditional products in keeping families alive.

Jak fruit is one of the most popular garden crops commonly grown and processed by rural women from different ethnic backgrounds in Sri Lanka. It is consumed directly as cooked food, as ripe fresh fruit and in a variety of preparations in processed forms. The *jak* fruit trees, which grow in most parts of the country, also provide timber, leaves for animal food, and wood for fuel.

Processing of *jak* fruit

Mature *jak* fruits are selected for processing. First, the fruit is usually cut into four portions for easy handling, the centre core chopped out and the seeds and flesh separated. The flesh (known as 'bulbs') and the seeds are then processed separately in either blanched or raw form, using different techniques. Women stress that it is important that no washing is done at any stage in processing, as exposure to additional moisture would have negative effects on sun-drying, a major technique used in *jak* processing.

Sun-drying of blanched *jak* flesh

The stages of drying the fruit are: slicing, blanching, draining and drying. Women

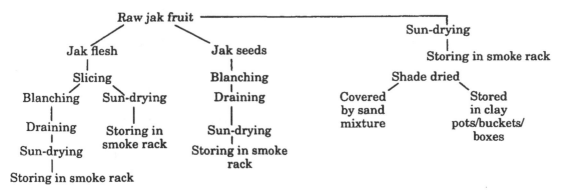

Figure 5. Processing of *jak* fruit

Table 1. Food composition of *jak* fruit (per 100g produce, raw weight)

Nutrients	Measure	Jak bulbs	Jak seeds
Energy	KCal	51	151
Proteins	g	2.6	4.3
Fats	g	0.3	0.4
Carbohydrates	g	9.4	32.6
Calcium	mg	30.0	35.0
Phosphorus	mg	40.0	126.0
Iron	mg	1.7	1.2
Vitamin A	µg	Nil	Nil
Carotene	µg	Nil	25.0
Thiamine	µg	50.0	180.0
Riboflavin	µg	40.0	50.0
Niacin	mg	2.0	0.5
Vitamin C	mg	14.0	17.5
Moisture	g	84.0	70.0

Source: Extract from food consumption tables – Medical Institute, Sri Lanka.

slice the *jak* bulbs using a knife, but prefer tearing them with their fingers as they say it minimizes shrivelling. The fruits are sliced lengthwise or crosswise according to their maturity: over-ripe fruit are cut crosswise to facilitate quick drying, which is a critical factor in the handling.

The cut slices are immersed in boiling water for a short time, which is called blanching. Blanching time depends on the 'starchiness' of the fruit, which women estimate from their knowledge of the trees from which the fruits are collected. Women say that starchy fruits require less blanching and they use the 'finger nail' test to decide the blanching time needed, which is a critical factor in the quality of the finished product. By pressing a finger nail against the fruit, women judge whether it is ready: 'it should be firm but still a little soft'.

Variation of methods among different groups of women

Some women maintain that steaming is an improvement over blanching, as the indirect contact with water reduces the moisture content and allows more control in achieving the desired extent of blanching. The use of salt during blanching also shows variation among different ethnic groups of women, according to their priorities. Most Tamil women add salt to the blanching water as they believe that in addition to its taste, salt acts as a preservative. On the other hand, some Sinhalese women caution against the use of too much salt which can make the product soggy and encourage the growth of mildew. Tamil women also add saffron to boiling water, both for colour and as an insect repellent.

The blanched fruit is then put into a *kirigotta*, a large strainer made out of a local reed, to allow water to drain out. The aim is to reduce the moisture content as much as possible before sun-drying it. Drying is done on a variety of surfaces, depending on the locality. Flat rocks are preferred as they retain the heat from the sun. Reed mats, dried woven coconut branches, palmyra leaves (in Jaffna), jute sacks and clean zinc sheets may also be used. Some women use a low table, the surface of which is made of thin wooden strips placed at intervals of three inches, which allows air to circulate freely and speeds up drying.

Tamil women use margosa leaf as an insect repellent during the sun-drying of the fruit. Other women use lime leaves or lemon rind, or particular herbs. Drying takes between two to four days, depending on the weather. Sound and colour are significant factors in assessing adequate drying. Women test for *kara-kara gaanawa* – a crackling sound – when they run their hands through the pieces, or a sound known as *takas* when broken in two. Difficulty in biting on it is also a test used by some to assess whether sufficiently dried.

Storage

The dried fruit will stay in good condition for a period of four to six months. The *duma*, the smoke chamber built immediately above the cooking hearth, just below the smoke escape chimney, is crucial to the storage of the fruit, as it exposes the dry products to heat and smoke. Women prefer to store the fruit in clay pots covered with thick paper, but will also use jute sacks, woven baskets, tins and, more recently, paper bags.

Women maintain that processed food should not be used until at least four weeks after the end of the drying, and that the products need to be handled hygienically to reduce the risk of spoilage.

Sun-drying of raw (unboiled) *jak* fruit is less complicated but less popular because its success is more dependent on good weather. Women use this method occasionally to save time, but emphasize that cutting the fruit into very fine slices is important to achieve quick drying. The product cannot be stored as long.

Processing of *jak* seeds

Jak seeds are also processed as blanched or raw. The processing of blanched seeds is very similar to that of blanched fruit, with different tests being used to determine blanching and drying adequacy.

Processing of raw *jak* seeds uses sand. The seeds of mature fruit are first dried in the shade and then layered with sand either in a corner of the kitchen, or in a cavity in the mud floor. The sand used is a special mixture of dried river sand and ant-hill clay, known as *humbas mati*. Some women may also use containers – large clay pots, discarded galvanized buckets and wooden boxes – for processing the seeds. Most women make tiered arrangements in individual clusters, each comprising about one hundred *jak* seeds. This enables the users to take out only the required quantity of seeds without disturbing the rest.

Food security

For poorer rural women, processing *jak* fruit is a means of meeting urgent food security needs. During the off-season, rural women use processed *jak* fruit at least three times a week either to supplement the main meal of rice or at times as a substitute for the staple. Women maintain that, when the demand for casual labour falls during the rainy season putting them in situations of dire poverty, such foods help to 'fill their stomachs'.

Organization of fruit processing

Women stress the importance of organization and planning in *jak* fruit process-

ing. All the related processing activities should follow in a rapid sequence, as delay in any particular phase could adversely affect the finished product. The first step is to create enough time to carry out the processing: women will cook extra rice the night before and prepare it for breakfast with chilli to save time from cooking in the morning. Collecting extra fuelwood and water, borrowing large cooking pots from friends and sunning the large mats used for drying are all among the various preparatory activities leading to the processing day. If the children are on holiday from school they will help as well.

During processing, women adapt their techniques to cope with unexpected climatic conditions or demands on their time. If they are unable to get through the slicing work in time for the sunniest part of the day, they prefer to cut the fruit in chunks since the larger pieces of raw fruit can be kept overnight without spoiling. If, by the time slicing is finished, the sunlight is inadequate for drying, the raw fruit is spread on thick sheets of paper to be placed on the smoke rack in the kitchen so that the product does not spoil and drying can begin. When the sun is bright enough, the slices are taken outdoors. Working at low levels of technology where the women have no control over certain factors, they constantly adapt their indigenous techniques to achieve the best results. (Abeywardane, 1990)

Smoke in Sudanese women's culture

Little is known about women's traditional techniques of coping with difficulties in their environments – not only in food production and processing, but also in other areas such as building materials and health.

Smoke has such a special place in female Sudanese culture that there are two names for it in the local Arabic: *Ussab* indicates normal firewood smoke, like that issued during cooking, or *dukhan* when it is intended for a useful end.

While many African women may be aware of the good-smelling smoke that is used to smoke a room or a drinking-water pot, the many other ways that the Sudanese women use *dukhan* from a variety of trees is unknown elsewhere in the region.

Umra as a preservative and pasteurizing agent for milk

The most common purpose for which women utilize *dukhan* is the smoking of two milk containers. One of these, a milking basket called an *umra* or *kahal*, has been made by women out of palm leaves, probably for thousands of years. The other one – the *bukhssa* – is a gourd in which soured milk is churned to produce butter.

Special types of wood are used to produce the smoke needed. In the case of the *umra* for instance, wood from *sarob*, *tundub* or *kitir* is used. The *umra* is never washed, and when smoked just before milking it reaches a temperature of 80°C for a few minutes. The milk traces covering the inside surface of the utensil burn, turning into a plastic-like layer which seals the pores of the wickerwork basket. This layer is impregnated with chemicals from the smoke which, together with the raised temperature during processing, have a preservative effect. Milk kept in the *umra* does not spoil as easily as milk kept in non-smoked containers, and the pleasant smoky flavour is regarded as an added advantage.

The gourd, used both for souring and churning, sometimes develops a bad flavour and a bitter taste due to growth of the wrong kinds of bacteria. In this case, women thoroughly clean the gourd with water, dry it in the sun and then smoke it before souring a new batch with the help of a good starter, such as a little sour milk.

Smoke as a construction material

The nomadic Hadendowa women in eastern Sudan live in homes consisting of a tent made from large doum palm leaf mats called *birish*. A new *birish*, which is whitish in colour, is very susceptible to microbial decay when it gets wet during the rainy season. At the same time water can easily penetrate the pores making everything inside the tent wet as well.

During the months preceding the rains, women dismantle the tents, fold each *birish* and smoke it until it turns dark. This smoked *birish* is no longer susceptible to microbial decay during the rains. The smoke has several effects: first the microbes that are already present on the mat are killed through the prolonged smoking process; second, the mats are impregnated with smoke chemicals that probably have a residual effect which lasts at least through the rainy season; third, the pores of the mat are sealed with carbon particles and chemicals. The outside surface of the tent becomes nonporous and smooth, so that the raindrops roll away before they have a chance to soak through the mat.

Women smoke themselves for their babies

Sudanese women not only smoke various materials, but they also smoke themselves. A small smoke pit, *hufrat el subagh* found in almost every traditional Sudanese house is used for this purpose. A special kind of wood, *talih* (acacia) or shaff wood, obtained from the tree called *el subagh*, is burnt in this small pit to generate the smoke. Women sit on a special palm leaf mat with a central opening placed over the pit and cover themselves with a locally made blanket – *shamla* – to contain the smoke. The process is a harsh one and women have to withstand the high temperature for about 15–20 minutes.

Women with newborn babies are encouraged by older women to smoke themselves, since it is believed that the smoke particles enter the mother's breasts and the milk is good for the healthy growth of the baby. Children who develop bacterial infections during the teething period, resulting in vomiting and diarrhoea, are invariably treated by smoking as well. The mother, after smoking herself, scrapes the sweat which contains the smoke particles from her body, and presses it against the child's gums and rubs its whole body with it. Moreover, women who smoke themselves are said not to develop skin diseases or vaginal infections. Although some doctors claim that smoking could possibly cause vaginal cancer, there has been no research on the subject so far.

Women carry the smoke with them

It is not always convenient for women, especially nomadic women who apparently developed the culture and the various techniques of smoking, to smoke themselves. They have therefore devised a way by which they can carry the smoke with them: the smoke chemicals are trapped in a special sorghum-grain-based cosmetic cream called *dilka*. *Dilka* is found in all homes, and is used especially by brides.

A paste of sorghum is stuck to the bottom of a wide, wooden or metal bowl, which is then inverted over the smoke pit mentioned above. The process is repeated for three days every now and then, with the paste being kneaded by hand and mixed with various perfumes. The paste produced in the end is a moist product with a dark colour as a result of the smoke chemicals and the heating process. This product, if well made, keeps for years without spoiling: it is acidic, has low water activity and is impregnated with smoke chemicals.

Women, and at times men, also use the *dilka* by rubbing and massaging it into the whole naked body. When children in rural Sudan develop food poisoning, they are often given water to drink in which a small piece of *dilka* has been suspended.

Despite the amazing range and complexity of its uses, women's smoke technology in Sudan has never been documented; the nature of this ancient technology, its potential as well as its limits and possible drawbacks remain unexplored. Does this lack of interest derive from the fact that it is 'indigenous women's stuff'? *(based on interview with Prof. Hamid Dirar, Faculty of Agriculture, Khartoum, Sudan, 1991)*

Potato production in the Andes

This case study illustrates the extent of the knowledge that women farmers have regarding seed diversity.

A few of the old women farmers in the Quechua Communities who live in the Andes possess rare knowledge of plant breeding which was probably a legacy of the ancient Inca civilization. The younger generations so far have not emulated the role of the older farmers as 'curators of diversity'.

Potatoes are normally propagated by asexual reproduction, by planting whole potatoes or sections. The resulting plants are 'clones', i.e. they have identical characteristics to their 'parent' potato. A few of the women farmers in the province of Cuzco, however, use true potato seeds, a practice which has been all but abandoned. They have learned this method of propagation from older women peasants who would come to their community from the highlands to help with the harvest. The highland peasants told the Quechua women about the 'berry' on the potato plant and the seeds inside.

Since the Andes Mountains are the place of origin of the potato, there are countless varieties, and people have different uses for each type. Using seeds for progagation, Andean women are able to breed new varieties with characteristics which they themselves choose. Before harvesting the potato crop, the women collect the berries and store them in a large ceramic bowl outside the house where they remain until the following October. By then they have become black and rotten. Allowing the berries to rot before planting the seeds is an essential part of the process – it produces the chemicals which activate the dormant seeds for germination.

The seeds are planted just before the rains and the plants are maintained just until they produce tiny tubers. The products of this harvest, 'grandchildren' of the berry seeds, will be used for 'tuber seeds'. Women sort the 'tuber seeds' by shape and colour; normally there are more than 12 types. These are usually distributed among their children to be planted to produce food crops, while some are given away in sets as wedding presents to help young couples start cultivation. (Ojeda, undated)

Section II
Women's local technological innovation

Cassava processing in Luwero District, Uganda

Women's innovative capacities can be the key to survival in times of disaster

Ugandan women use the whole cassava plant not only as a food crop, but for firewood, cooking oil, medicine and building material, and as a source of cash income. Certain properties of cassava, such as its tolerance of drought, poor soil and neglect, and the fact that it can be stored underground for several months after maturation, make this crop an important food source for rural populations in semi-subsistence economies in sub-Saharan Africa, particularly in times of food shortage. It is an excellent source of dietary energy and is traditionally prepared by women with protein-rich foods. However, although cassava constitutes one-third of the total production of cereals, roots and plantains in the region, it is often seen as a low-status or poverty food.

Cassava has not traditionally been a popular food in Uganda, but by the mid-1980s, when years of civil war had wiped out most other crops in the country, it was one of the few available foodstuffs. When people, mainly widows and orphans, returned to their villages at the end of the war, they found that the only crop they could grow was cassava, which had remained in the ground. Women have since developed ways of utilizing every bit of this plant for a whole range of uses.

Cassava roots normally do not store for more than a few days after digging. They are usually dug up, peeled and then cooked, mostly with beans or meat, and eaten immediately. For longer term preservation women usually slice and dry the cassava into tablets, which they store in sacks and pots, or mill it into flour. Women use the processed cassava for home consumption particularly during the dry season when fresh food is not readily available, or is too expensive to buy. The dried cassava tablets last at the most four months before they require further drying. A new product that women in Luwero have developed recently is *mawogo nkyenka* – cassava pellets – which keep for longer periods if packed. *Mawogo nkyenka* cassava pellets, made out of grated, dried and fried cassava, are ready-to-use all year round. Women use these pellets to prepare breakfast by adding boiled milk and sugar; as a snack by mixing them with roasted groundnuts, simsim or soybeans; and finally as a proper meal by moistening them with clean water and adding them to other foods like minced meat, fish or bean sauce. The production of these pellets is limited, however, due to poor grating facilities. There is room for improvement of the grating technology for increased production and also for upgrading the techniques for even longer preservation of cassava food products.

Marketing cassava products

Women use flour made from the sweet variety of cassava as a much cheaper and readily available alternative to wheat flour, to prepare cakes and cookies, and to develop other new products for the market. They have succeeded in popularizing some of these, such as *kabalagala*, a kind of pancake made out of a mixture of cassava flour, sweet bananas, pepper and oil which is fried. Women who live around rural schools can earn their living by selling *kabalagala* at break-time. Some women, either as individuals or in cooperatives, bake cakes for parties, or biscuits which can be packed and stored for long-term use.

Enguli – a new product and source of cash

After the war, women adapted their traditional brewing technology for the production of the local alcoholic drink – *enguli* – from cassava, the only raw product in abundance at the time. In its processed form *enguli* is a colourless liquid that is a mixture of alcohols. Women sell it to breweries which further process it into a more refined drink, Uganda gin or Uganda *waragi*.

Cassava tubers are dug out of the soil, peeled, chopped into pieces and dried. The dried product is pounded by women who are sometimes assisted by their daughters. Water is added and the mixture is kept in a pit to ferment. Meanwhile maize seeds are allowed to germinate, and are dried and then pounded. The fermented cassava is fried in a pan to a brown colour, and water and the pounded maize seeds are added to the mixture, which is then left to ferment further.

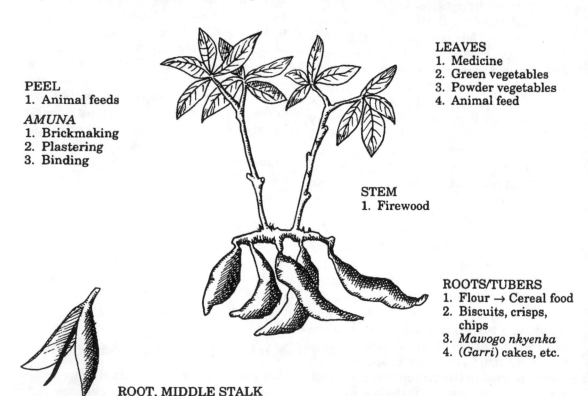

PEEL
1. Animal feeds

AMUNA
1. Brickmaking
2. Plastering
3. Binding

LEAVES
1. Medicine
2. Green vegetables
3. Powder vegetables
4. Animal feed

STEM
1. Firewood

ROOTS/TUBERS
1. Flour → Cereal food
2. Biscuits, crisps, chips
3. *Mawogo nkyenka*
4. (*Garri*) cakes, etc.

ROOT, MIDDLE STALK
1. Scientific laboratory tests

Figure 6. Ugandan women utilize every part of the cassava plant to produce a wide range of essential products

The fermented mixture is squeezed and filtered, giving a brown liquid and a sticky yellowish residue. This residue constitutes an important animal feed in Luwero (see below). Women distil the brown liquid by heating it in drums on wood fires. The vapour is led through tubes cooled in water and finally condensed in a container. This condensed colourless liquid is *enguli*.

Marketing and further processing of *enguli*

The village women sell the *enguli* to men in the local markets. Despite the small scale of most women's production, the income generated is such that even single mothers can afford basic expenses such as school fees. The importance of the cash income from *enguli* sales can be understood better within the context of low-income areas such as the Luwero District, where 70 per cent of the population are widows and orphans. Some women manage to operate on a larger scale, marketing the locally-prepared gin to some national distilleries. Quality is an important factor in selling to the larger distilleries. The local brew, which is simply stored in sealed cans for transportation to towns, is bought by the distilleries if it is at least 40 per cent alcohol. Distillers carry out the final refinement by eliminating impurities and adding flavours.

Utilization of *enguli* by-products

Women also utilize many of the *enguli* by-products in the following ways:
Animal feed: the yellow residue that remains after the initial squeezing and filtration of the cassava during *enguli* production, as mentioned earlier, is the main source of animal feed in the area. Indeed, the village women in Luwero report that all the pigs and chickens that they rear flourish on this feed.

Amuna: another useful by-product of *enguli* production is called *amuna*, a viscous liquid that remains in the distillation tank as a residue. Women have found that this residue, which can be easily drained out of the drums, is an efficient and cheap substitute for cement. Now most women in Luwero have reduced the dependence on cement and lime in some cases by completely replacing them with *amuna* for brickmaking, plastering, joining bricks during construction, and floor-making.

Preservative: women who use cassava flour to produce cakes, biscuits, pancakes and other such products for sale to the market, use *enguli* as a preservative in these foods. Given its high alcohol content, *enguli* acts as an effective preservative.

Other uses of cassava

The women utilize every bit of the cassava to meet other important needs as well. The cassava leaves, for instance, when washed in salty water, dried and pounded to powder can be kept for over two years. This powder, called *gobe*, is mixed with petroleum jelly and used as a cure for skin rashes. The leaves also provide a good alternative to iodine or spirits for use on fresh wounds. They are washed, chopped, mixed with a little salt, and the paste is tied around the wound with a bandage. *Gobe* is also used as a condiment with groundnut soup.

Dried and pounded cassava makes a strong glue when heated. Another technique for making glue is using pieces of cloth or perforated sacks to press the white starchy liquid out of cassava. The glue is formed by heating the starch.

Women use some starch residue for cooking or selling to laboratories, for use in the textile industry or village tailoring projects. The glue, on the other hand, is sold to local shopkeepers, who use it making paper bags, or to distilleries that use it to attach labels to *waragi* bottles. (Simwogerere, 1991; Onabolu, 1988)

Nkejje fish in Lake Victoria, Uganda

Ignoring women's traditional knowledge and use of different foods can lead to environmental, economic and social disasters. Nevertheless, women continue to make the best use of their available resources to adapt and innovate in difficult situations. This case study also highlights the issue of scientists 'rediscovering' local women's knowledge.

For the people living along the shores of Lake Victoria, in the Jinja District of Uganda, fishing has traditionally had a very important role in the economic, social and cultural aspects of their lives. Women make use of the many species of fish which exist in this huge area of fresh water to ensure the health of their families.

The *nkejje* fish is of particular importance in preventing malnutrition and related childhood diseases. This small fish, with an average size of three inches, contains 56.4 per cent protein and 11 per cent fat, with a high calcium content.

The women of Jinja have traditionally been involved in the fishing itself as well as processing fish products. Traditional fishing gear consisted of lift baskets, swim traps or scooping baskets. Women would weave this equipment out of papyrus, treebark, banana fibres and creepers and use them in shallow waters. To catch the *nkejje* fish, women used rectangular floats to which they would attach a special thorny shrub whose ash would attract the *nkejje* as it fell in the water.

As modern fishing technology has replaced traditional equipment, women's sphere of activity has become limited to the processing of the fish. Women prepare and preserve most of the local fish by covering it in banana leaves, peels or grass and smoking it. The low fat content of the *nkejje*, however, makes it suitable for sun-drying. Women prepare a clean rock surface on which they place the *nkejje* for sun-drying, covering it with grass to preserve the flavour and also to protect it against direct exposure to sunlight. The drying process continues at night because of the heat radiating from the rock surface.

Traditionally the *nkejje* fish is believed to be a particularly good cure for measles. 'There is no better treatment,' says an old woman from Jinja, 'the *nkejje* is boiled and the child can drink the water and get better.' However, the women of the Jinja District are now faced with a severe shortage of the *nkejje* fish.

The introduction, in 1965, of Nile perch and tilapia into Lake Victoria, under a scheme supported by the Ugandan Government and two international development agencies has led to serious social, economic and ecological changes. There was little local participation in this programme, and a foreign fishery expert had advised that the *nkejje* fish should be left to die of old age, and instead the production of the 'more profitable' Nile perch promoted. The Nile fish fed on the *nkejje* almost to the point of making it extinct. While the commercial catch of the Nile fish increased from 0.42 per cent in 1981 to 55.0 per cent in 1985, that of *nkejje* fell from 96.38 per cent in 1981 to zero in 1985.

Increased algal activity is among the most alarming ecological imbalances

**Figure 7. Tradi-
tional fishing gear
made and used by
women in Uganda**

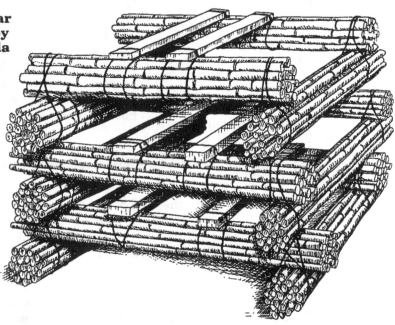

occurring in the lake. The plankton, which were normally fed on by the *nkejje*, have been free to grow without check. Due to changes in the distribution of these plankton, an algal bloom may flourish, causing the lake to look green and making the water less safe to drink. It is also common to see dead fish on the surface of the water, asphyxiated by the algae. The big Nile perch processing plants that have been set up around the lake are another pollution threat in the area. Being dependent on the high-protein *nkejje* to combat malnutrition in their children, low-income mothers particularly have suffered from the scarcity of the fish. The higher fat content of the Nile perch makes it less easy for children to digest and furthermore local people do not like the taste.

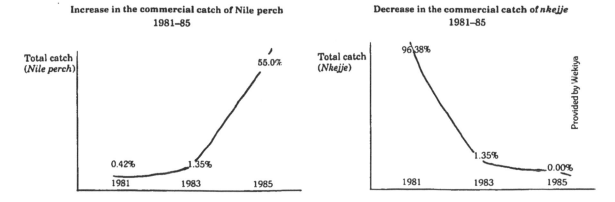

Figure 8. The Nile fish fed on the *nkejje* almost to the point of making it extinct

Women respond to change

In the midst of the changes following the introduction of the Nile fish into Lake Victoria, the Jinja women have developed innovative ways of dealing with the new circumstances. In order to make the now scarce *nkejje* last, after drying the fish, it is pounded to a powder using a mortar and pestle or a grinding stone, and sieved. The *nkejje*, once dried and powdered, can be stored for long periods, and will last much longer as it is added in small amounts to baby and other foods.

The *nkejje* needs to be very dry in order to allow for easy pounding, which means that women cannot wash it after the drying process is complete. Hence the *nkejje* laid outside for sun-drying needs greater care to keep it clean. In order to assure the hygiene of the product women have now started washing the fish thoroughly immediately after catching. They then stack the fish on sticks passed through their gills and lay them out on papyrus mats made especially for the clean drying of the *nkejje*. Seeing the demand for

the ever-decreasing *nkejje* fish, various entrepreneurs have taken up the local women's idea of powdering the fish. Some small production firms using locally fabricated driers and hammer mills have been set up in the area. Today it is possible to walk into any grocery store and buy *nkejje* powder.

Women lose ownership of their knowledge

The traditional importance that women attach to the *nkejje* recently prompted some research into the fish, which resulted in the discovery of its high protein and calcium content. Protein supports the immune system and hence improves a child's resistance to potentially dangerous diseases such as measles. The discovery led to nutrition clinics using *nkejje* in the treatment of various childhood diseases, and ironically to a strong government campaign to encourage mothers to feed their children with *nkejje*. The knowledge which the women have been utilizing for many years is

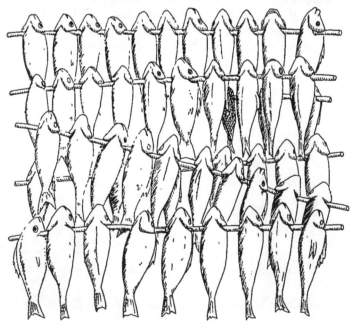

Figure 9. *Nkejje* **fish stacked on sticks for sun-drying**

now being offered back to them as 'scientific' knowledge.

There is growing recognition by the policy makers that decreasing *nkejje* supplies might lead to significant problems for many poor households in the area. Recently the Minister of Agriculture, Animal Industry and Fisheries, one of the woman ministers in the cabinet, appealed to the public to save the *nkejje* and banned the use of fishing nets with small holes. Such measures are intended to reverse the adverse effects of the introduction of the Nile perch, exacerbated by advanced fishing technologies such as powered boats and large nylon nets which allow indiscriminate fishing. Despite such compensatory policies, however, the government continues to support the Nile fish processing and export companies.

To ensure lasting supplies of the *nkejje*, the women of the Jinja Municipality have recently asked the Uganda Fresh Fisheries Research Organisation (UFFRO) for assistance to grow the fish in artificial ponds that would be controlled by a woman's co-operative. UFFRO has promised technical assistance to the women on the condition that the pond would be within the reach of the research station. Following this, the women applied to the Jinja Municipal Council for land, only to receive the response 'You get fish from the Lake, why make your own pond?' (Wekiya, 1991)

Salt extraction in Sierra Leone

Sierra Leonean women's scientific knowledge and innovative capacities are helping to meet the country's demand for salt.

A common joke in Sierra Leone explains the significant place that salt holds in the country. The joke says that the Konos (an ethnic group occupying the eastern part of the country) sold their birthright for salt to the Mendes (a neighbouring ethnic

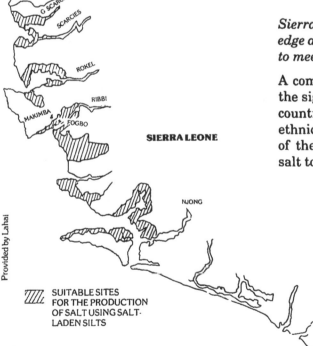

SUITABLE SITES FOR THE PRODUCTION OF SALT USING SALT-LADEN SILTS

Provided by Lahai

Figure 10. Most of the salt consumed in Sierra Leone is imported while the long coastline of the country could potentially facilitate large-scale salt production if women salt producers were to be supported

group) and since then have become the slaves of the Mendes. Indeed salt is an indispensable item for Sierra Leoneans, not only in food preparation, but also in fish, meat and oil preservation, as well as in the treatment of wounds.

Sierra Leone has no organized salt processing industry and relies mostly on imported salt from Senegal and on small-scale producers in the informal sector, who are all women. It is estimated that only about 35 per cent of the salt consumed in Sierra Leone is of local origin despite the long coastline in the country which could facilitate large-scale salt production. The foreign exchange crisis that the country is facing now is bound to result in an increasing demand for locally-produced salt.

For most women living on the coastal lowlands, salt-processing is their primary occupation and the main source of income for their families during the dry season. Women join this informal industry as soon as they have come of age and they have usually mastered the difficult skills involved in producing a marketable product by their early 20s.

Women's innovations in salt processing

Originally Sierra Leonean women processed salt simply by boiling sea water

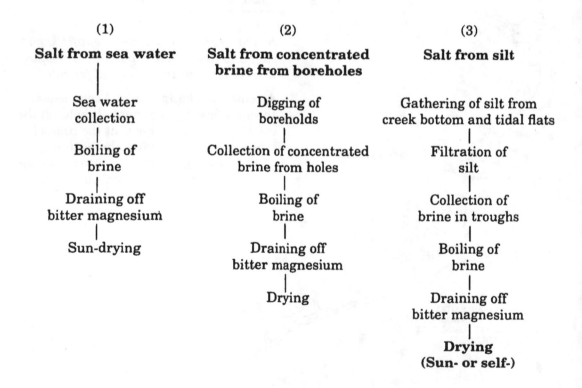

Figure 11. **Women's technological innovations in salt processing**

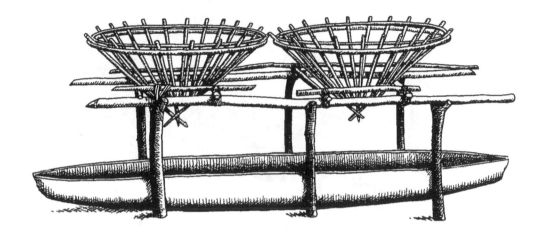

Figure 12. Wooden frame for the conical percolation funnel

in earthenware pots over traditional three-stone fires. Boiling was followed by sun-drying, and the operations took place in temporary huts built on beaches. However, the salt concentration of the sea water is low and therefore large quantities of brine had to be evaporated to produce small amounts of salt. Fuelwood consumption was also high.

These problems led women to the idea of collecting brine from ponds. To facilitate this, boreholes were dug along the tidal paths, which filled with brine during high tide. At low tide the brine was collected and evaporated until the salt crystallized. The salinity of the brine in the boreholes increased through seepage and solar evaporation leading to a shorter boiling time. The use of boreholes also overcame the problem of long and repeated journeys to the sea. Eventually women went on to develop a technique of extracting salt from silt, probably through the accidental discovery of salt crystals on the leaves and stems of the *bulei* tree (*Avicennia africana*) in the months of February and March. This observation led women to the discovery that the silt at the base of these trees was

laden with salt. This in turn led to the clearing of the vegetation to facilitate the collection of silt, and the subsequent extraction of salt from the silt.

In order to leach salt from the silt, women adapted the perforated baskets that are traditionally used by women soap makers. The salt-laden silt is collected from creek bottoms, mixed with sea water and left to separate in these baskets which serve as a percolation funnel when placed over wooden troughs in which the filtrate collects. The filtrate is then boiled on a protected three-stone fire in evaporating dishes until the salt crystallizes. The salt then is dried either in the sun or by heat from the fire.

In time women have changed the design of the perforated basket to a conical shape in response to technical difficulties. The perforated basket did not give very clear brine, which resulted in poor quality salt. The conical funnel on the other hand improved on the brine colour but, compared to the basket, had a low silt-holding capacity which slowed down the rate of filtration. Building a larger conical funnel in order to increase the silt-holding capacity posed some problems for the women.

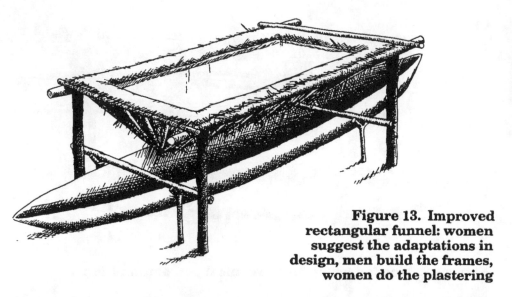

Figure 13. Improved rectangular funnel: women suggest the adaptations in design, men build the frames, women do the plastering

While men build the wooden frame for the funnel, women plaster it with mud in preparation for the filtration. Larger conical frames required women to assume physical positions that were almost impossible for them. Also, the women found that a larger funnel was less firm and therefore less efficient. Hence they suggested a rectangular design for the funnel which enabled a faster and more productive filtration.

The stoves used during the evaporation stage have also changed. The first adaptation was from the traditional three-stone open fire to the more efficient wall-protected fire which was designed by the women themselves. The second adaptation was a two-burner stove introduced by the Fourah Bay College. While this stove was a 50 per cent improvement over the open fire and a 35 per cent improvement over the wall-protected fire with respect to efficiency in fuelwood consumption, its adoption has been very low. This is partly due to the fact that it needed a blacksmith for maintenance and partly because it could not accommodate all types of cooking pots. The wall-protected fire, developed by the women themselves, is the most common design and is used by most processors. Apart from decreasing fuel consumption, it can accommodate any size or shape of evaporating dish.

Evaporating dishes have also changed. Women found that enamel basins gave much whiter salt than the traditional earthenware pots. The only disadvantage was the cost and sometimes the availability. Currently all salt processors use rectangular-shaped evaporating dishes made from scrap metal and drums. These are fabricated locally and therefore always available.

Technological skills involved in salt-from-silt extraction

The skill level of the operators of the salt-from-silt extraction technology is the most crucial element in determining the quality of the salt. Constructing an efficient funnel requires a very careful lining and plastering process. The boiling operation on the other hand involves skilful regulating of the fire, in order to facilitate the crystallization of pure salt (sodium chloride), while preventing the crystallization of bitter magnesium salts and the burning of the final product. The more

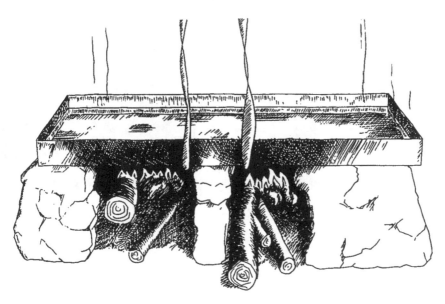

Figure 14. Wall-protected fire introduced by women for more fuel-efficient salt water boiling

experience a salt producer has, or the more skilled she is, the whiter and more pure is her salt. The acquisition of skills and knowledge in salt processing takes place within an informal context of information transfer from older to younger women, mostly within the same family. Born in a salt-processing community, most women master the various skills and procedures in salt processing through observation and practice. The sharing of information about new ideas, practices and technologies similarly takes place at an interpersonal level among the women producers. Inter-village marriages, visits between kin, and migration are among the factors that facilitate information sharing.

Salt processing as a woman's enterprise in Sierra Leone

The relatively low cost and year-round availability of locally-produced salt has attracted a lot of traders to the processing areas. As the foreign exchange deficit in

Sierra Leone continues to increase, the local production of salt is becoming more important. Relying mainly on local sources and expertise this industry has provided 35 per cent of the national need for salt. At the same time it provides employment to 1152 households in the area (excluding temporary processors) and thousands more involved in salt trading. The only government attempt so far at local salt production has been a short-lived attempt at a large-scale solar salt works at Suen. It failed mainly due to environmental and technical problems. People's, and in this case women's, technology however, has survived, adapting to changing circumstances and becoming more efficient. (Lahai, 1991; Massaquoi, 1990)

Women potters in Kenya

Women potters use their knowledge and skills to adapt to rapidly changing markets and a crisis in the supply of fuelwood.

Provided by Mutagaywa

Clay can be kneaded by hand or by foot   **Coiling**

Figure 15. Kneading and shaping a pot

In Western Kenya, pottery has traditionally been the woman's domain.
Women produce various types of pots and
pans mainly for household use, in food
processing, preparation, and storage. In
the Luo area, for instance, the traditional
repertoire of pottery forms consisted of 12
different types.

The distribution of surplus pottery production was originally limited only to a
small geographical area. Due to the increasing economic significance of pottery
in recent times, however, pottery has become a major means of livelihood for the
women in the area.

The process of production

Women potters, who mostly live in the
Western Provinces of Kenya covering the
Kakamega, Kisumu, Siaya and Nyanza
Districts, collect the clay from communal
lands along the rivers, free of charge. The
top layer of earth is removed to expose
and dig up the good clay. Different clay

sources provide different types of clay,
and the women potters can tell the
various properties of certain types of clay
by colour and where it came from.

In the Kisumu District, women use the
clay immediately after they have dug it
out from the source. In Nyanza, Siaya and
Kakamega Districts, it is stored in a cool
place out of direct sunlight for a week or
two before use. Women know by experience the proportions by which the various
colour clays are to be mixed for different
purposes. The Umba Women's Group in
Siaya, for instance, collect three different
types of clay at the foot of *Got Ramogi*
(Ramogi Hill) which they dry and then
grind into a fine powder to be mixed with
water before use. The potters carefully
knead the clay using either their feet or
hands, adding a little water at a time.
When ready, the mixture is sorted for any
stones which are removed before starting
the shaping process.

Women use pot bottoms on which a
little dry soil from the homestead is

- o Simple open form: for processing and serving meat and vegetables (such as okra); or large sizes which are used for brewing and serving beer, or fermenting and serving porridge of millet/maize (such as *nyalora*).
- o Simple restricted form: for cooking and preparing fish (*haiga*); cooking and storing grains and starchy foods (*kabange* or *dakuon*).
- o Forms with a neck: to brew and store beer (*mbiru*); to carry and store water (*dapi*); for odd jobs (*agulu*).

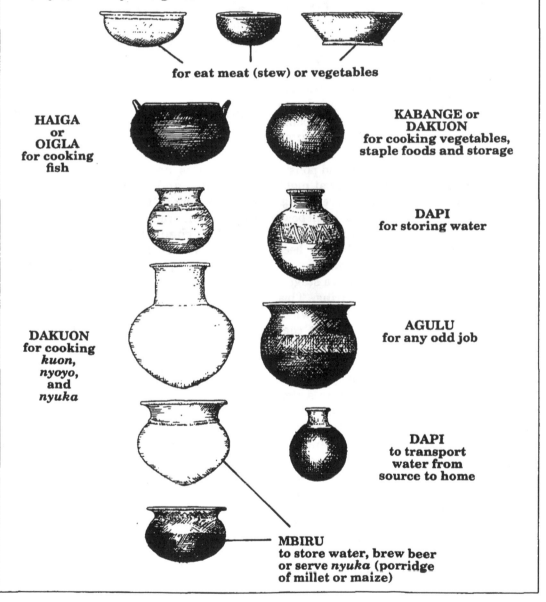

for eat meat (stew) or vegetables

HAIGA or OIGLA for cooking fish

KABANGE or DAKUON for cooking vegetables, staple foods and storage

DAPI for storing water

DAKUON for cooking *kuon*, *nyoyo*, and *nyuka*

AGULU for any odd job

DAPI to transport water from source to home

MBIRU to store water, brew beer or serve *nyuka* (porridge of millet or maize)

Figure 16. Traditional pottery forms in Luo, Kenya

sprinkled. The clay is pressed into the bottom to form a new pot. Coils of approximately six to seven centimetres in diameter are prepared by hand and placed one at a time to form an integral part of the new port. Shaping is done at the end of this process and excess clay is scraped off. The pot is then sprinkled with water and smoothed by hand. Some parts of the pot are roughened on the surface by using braided papyrus. Using her hand, the potter rolls the braid onto the smooth, damp clay.

Other decorations are made while the clay is still damp. The finished pot is left to dry indoors for one to three weeks depending on its size. Slow drying is essential, and therefore the pot is kept in a cool place. Pots that need colouring and polishing are worked on inside a hut or at night when it is cool, one day before firing. Women use hematite powder, a small bowl of water and a smooth stone to polish the surface of a pot. Cooking pots and beer pots are polished without the powder.

Having completed all the above stages, the pots are now ready for firing. This takes place on a dry day at a time when the direction of the wind is fairly constant, usually in the afternoon. On the firing day, dry pots are put out in the sun in the morning. Stones or old potsherds (pieces of broken pot) are placed in a ring on the ground where the pots are to be fired. Within this ring, dry twigs and grass, pots, firewood, wet twigs and dry leaves are placed in alternate layers. The pyre is thatched carefully with layers of dry grass. Wet grass cut on the same day is finally placed on the top and the pyre is ready for lighting. Two people kindle the fire in several places around the bottom running in opposite directions. Whenever an opening is noticed during the firing, it is immediately covered with fresh wet grass. A constant watch is required while firing, and more grass is used as required

until the potters feel that their pots are ready. Smoke blackens the inside of the pots, helping to seal the surface. As the fire burns out, the red hot pots are left standing on the stones and potsherds.

Cooking pots are exposed to traditional proofing using extracts of plants. Bark from special trees, such as the acacia tree, are soaked in water for about a week and boiled on the day of firing. The extract is a reddish-brown liquid. The liquid is sprinkled on the hot pots immediately when they are removed from the burned-out fire.

Transfer of skills and knowledge

Although pottery is the major income source for many women in Western Kenya, it is not a full-time occupation. The skills and knowledge are passed through generations, as well as among the different regions and tribes, through informal channels of communication. Older and more experienced women tend to teach younger ones – mother to daughter, mother-in-law to daughter-in-law, aunt to niece, and so on – mainly through observation and working together. As the older women reach the point when they can no longer see well, the younger generation takes over and keeps the skills and knowledge alive. The two main tribes who live in the area are the Luo and the Luhya. The Luo are Nilotics who are the traditional potters. Inter-marriage between the Luo and Luhya has been the main channel for the transfer of pottery skills from the former to the latter. Today, young women moving to other regions via marriage still take their skills with them and continue to transfer knowledge.

Innovations to meet new markets

The appearance of modern aluminium pots for cooking, and jerry cans for fetching water, and the gradual abandonment of traditional practices in food preparation have threatened markets for the traditional potters. Women have responded to these changes by innovating a wider range of products in order to secure their cash income. In response to changing eating habits, women have started producing ceramic casseroles for oven cooking, nonstick frying pans for cooking newly-popular foods like chapati, and shallower, flat-bottomed pots for cooking meat and vegetables on the stoves used in urban areas. They have also started producing decorative flower and plant pots, used in tourist hotels and big buildings in the cities, as well as lampshades, candlesticks, ashtrays and other ornamental pottery.

National policies have not helped the women. For example, the Lake Basin Development Authority's decision to clear the vegetation in the area, including papyrus, in order to make space for large-scale farming of irrigated high-value crops, has worked to the disadvantage of women potters. As a woman cannot own land or cut down trees in her own garden, the potters are dependent on the papyrus in these communal areas to use as firewood. In addition, the basket-weavers and mat-makers in the area who are also dependent on papyrus as their raw material have been made poorer.

Owing to increasing economic hardship, women have also adapted the organization of their productive activities. While traditionally women potters have worked individually, now they are forming pottery groups through which they attempt to maximize their resources, as well as minimize the risk factor of individual small-scale enterprise. There are also environmental factors, such as the severe shortage of fuelwood, that have led women to reorganize their productive activities in groups. For instance, now women use communal fires rather than individual ones to reduce fuelwood consumption.

Innovations in the type and range of pottery products have resulted in a competitive market for the women. Women living close to urban areas have often been able to improve their businesses. For women who live in remote rural areas, however, transportation is a major constraint in marketing their goods.

Some women's groups are now beginning to apply their skills to new activities, such as the production of ceramic liners for charcoal-burning stoves and fuel-efficient wood-burning stoves. There has been technical assistance from NGOs, supporting women potters in the innovative use of their traditional knowledge and skills. The demand for fuel-efficient stoves and liners is growing because of the general shortage of fuelwood, which means that their production is a potentially lucrative business. The users of the stoves state that they save time, money and energy, and are also safer when children are around. (Mutagaywa, 1991)

Survival skills of Tonga women in Zimbabwe

Tonga women's skills at recognizing and using indigenous 'wild' foods are now keeping families alive, and yet are unrecognized outside the area.

The silos are full, but stomachs are empty: this is Zimbabwe's food security paradox. Year after year there are reports that people are dying of starvation in some parts of Zimbabwe. One such area is Binga District, which is characterized by poor soils, erratic rainfall and the presence of wild animals. The Tonga tribe, who are inhabitants of this area, originally lived along the Zambezi River and its tributaries, farming the rich alluvial soils which were annually flooded by the

river. In 1957, however, the tribe was for-
cibly moved from the Zambezi River area
to the escarpment to make space for construction of the Kariba Lake Dam and
hydro-electric scheme.

When the Tonga were moved, their
whole farming system was disrupted, to
the extent that their survival was threatened. Binga District in Matabeleland
North Province, where most of the Tonga
resettled, is considered to be the poorest
in Zimbabwe in terms of soil conditions
and rainfall; there are no lakes for fishing, while because of the Natural Conservation Areas law, hunting is prohibited.
The levels of agricultural production are
not adequate to sustain food security for
average households of seven members
throughout the year, and the district is
classified as a food deficit area. The
drought relief which the government
issues year after year is inadequate, and
does not always get to the area because of
poor communications infrastructure.

Tonga women innovate and adapt for food security

Through the years the Tonga people have
devised methods of coping with harsh environmental conditions. Tonga women, who
are responsible for providing food for the
family and the community, innovated and
adapted food production and processing
technologies, and identified new sources of
food. While the attempts by expatriates and
development agencies to promote drought-
tolerant crops have not yielded any significant results, Tonga women have managed
to identify, collect and process 47 indigenous plants whose leaves are used for relish, and over 100 tree species with a variety
of edible parts. Some examples:

o In January, February and March, when
   food, especially the traditional cereals,
   is in short supply, the women collect

cereals from certain types of indigenous
grasses and process these to produce a
meal which is used in place of sorghum,
millet or maize meals.

o Women have substituted the traditional morning meal of tea and bread
   with a porridge and a drink made from
   the fruit of the baobab tree. The oval
   shell of the baobab fruit is cracked open
   and seeds which are embedded in a
   whitish powdery pulp are either soaked
   or boiled and a porridge prepared in the
   usual way. The pulp is nutritious. Likewise the fruit of the baobab can be
   eaten on its own or used to prepare a
   refreshing drink which is also used to
   treat fevers. Women can also extract oil
   from the seeds of the baobab. The bark
   of the baobab is soft and can be
   pounded and burnt to ash which
   women use as a form of caustic soda in
   the preparation of other green vegetables. Women also use the bark to
   weave rope or mats, and sell them for
   cash income.

o Women use a wide variety of green vegetables as relish to accompany a thick
   maize, millet or sorghum porridge,
   called *sadza*. They also collect rainy season vegetables, sun-dry them on metal
   sheets, and store them in jute bags for
   consumption during the dry season.

Tamarind

One of the wild plants that the Tonga
women started utilizing for a variety of
purposes is tamarind (*Tamarindus indica*). Tamarind is a tropical evergreen
tree with a low, rounded crown, which
may grow up to 24m in height and bears
large quantities of pale brown pods, 10cm
or more in length. Although tamarind
grows and is cultivated throughout the
tropics and sub-tropics of the world and is
used for a variety of purposes, from medicine to fish preservation, it is hardly

A. Tamarind fruit

B. A flowering tamarind branch

A mature tamarind tree

Provided by Mpofu and Mpande

Figure 17. Given the low yields of other crops grown in the Binga District, such as maize, sorghum and millet, tamarind serves as an important food supplement

recognized as a useful plant in Zimbabwe. It is due to the Tonga women's knowledge and skills that tamarind has started being utilized in Binga District.

Women climb trees to collect the fruit, which they store in jute bags until the next harvest, a period of 12 months. The fruit is of high nutritional value and does not rot, which renders it especially valuable in drought-stricken areas, and women like to store large quantities of fruit for use in times of food shortage and when fruit is unavailable. The fruit is stored in traditional units which women make out of mud, slightly raised above ground level.

Women process tamarind in a number of ways for the following purposes:

○ as a flavouring agent with a pleasant sour taste that enlivens porridge made out of millet, sorghum or maize. Either the fruit or, in times of food shortage, the leaves are soaked and boiled;

○ as a substitute for commercially produced beverages such as tea and coffee,

Table 2. Nutritional composition of tamarind (%) compared to some other crops grown in the Binga District

	Tamarind pulp	Tamarind leaves	Maize	Sorghum
Protein	3.1	5.8	10.5	9.7
Fat	0.4	2.1	6.5	3.3
Carbohydrate	70.8	18.2	66.0	67.7
Water	20.0	70.5	14.5	9.5
Fibre	3.0	1.9	2.5	7.0
Minerals	2.1	1.5	1.5	–

which are frequently not available due to budgetary constraints or distance from retail outlets. Usually the ripe fruits are used, but when these are unavailable, women also collect the unripe fruits, soak and boil them and finally add ash to help neutralize their acidity, to make a pleasant drink which can be either drunk alone or added to porridge;

o as a snack food: the seeds, which have a high protein content, can be fried and eaten as a snack;

o as a substitute for, or addition to, scarce maize, sorghum or millet meals. Women collect the unripe fruit, soak and boil the seeds, pound them, and add them to cereals;

o as a medicine: concentrations of tamarind liquid may be used to cure gastrointestinal disorders in humans, and may also be added to animals' drinking water in the belief that it cures sleeping sickness caused by the tsetse fly (it is not known how effective this is);

o as a coagulant: the acidic liquid from tamarind and other wild fruits is used to curdle fresh milk, in the same way that other acids, such as acetic or citric acid, are used in laboratories.

Marketing initiatives by the Tonga women

The Tonga women have also realized the commercial potential of tamarind and other wild fruits, and have started marketing the fresh fruit by the roadside and at bus stops. They use this cash to purchase equipment, like metal pots and plates, needed in food preparation and processing. There is an unquantified market for tamarind in the urban areas amongst the Asian communities. The Asians are said to use agents who come into the area to barter the fruit with the women in exchange for clothing rather than paying cash, which makes it difficult to assess the mon-

etary value of tamarind. Women are aware of the existence of this market but have not identified strategies for dealing with it. Their concern is that once large-scale commercialization of tamarind picks up, they will lose control over the source of the fruit, and that this subsistence crop, an important part of their diet, will not be available to them anymore.

Extension services and the policy environment act as obstacles

As part of the community development programme, the extension services encourage women in Binga to grow nonindigenous commercial varieties of fruit and vegetables, which have a high market value. Such varieties usually do not tolerate well the high temperatures prevailing in most areas of Binga. Some women were observed to plant local vegetables outside the gardens along the fences. Asked why they planted the wild vegetables outside, the women said:

'The extension services want us to use the available land, water and labour for the high yielding, exotic varieties that they have given us. Therefore we think that they would not like us to cultivate wild plants inside the gardens. They do not see the local plants as important, although they are the ones that survive the high temperatures from September to November. By planting them alongside the fence we are able to water them at the same time as we are planting the garden, without getting ourselves into trouble with the extension workers.'

Despite the wide availability of tamarind in many rural areas of Zimbabwe, and its importance for the diets of many rural families living in areas of poor fertility, there is no recognition of the fruit by governmental or non-governmental organizations working in these places. On the contrary, in many cases they are actively promoting cash crops. Given the wide range of uses of tamarind in Asian, Latin American and other African countries, and the availability of processing technologies, there is potential for further development of tamarind use in Zimbabwe. Such development would be encouraged by the sharing of information between countries of the South. (Mpofu and Mpande, 1991)

Soybean *daddawa* in Nigeria

The dissemination of an innovation by Nigerian women has spread quickly due to its base in local knowledge and skills.

Throughout the West African Savanna, *daddawa* (a Hausa word, also *dawadawa*) or 'local maggi' is eaten regularly in soups and stews, usually together with dumplings and porridge made out of sorghum or millet. *Daddawa* is a protein-rich seasoning which is used like stock cubes or cheese in European and North American cooking. It gives taste to countless meals in the region in addition to improving the protein content. It is known as *soumbara* in French-speaking countries of West Africa, and has many local names as well.

Nigerian women play the major role in the processing and marketing of *daddawa* and its production at cottage-industry level and it provides income for thousands of women in the region. A considerable number of middle-men are also involved in the distribution of *daddawa* in Nigeria, as well as to other countries in West and Central Africa such as Cameroon, Chad and Niger Republic.

Traditional processing of *daddawa*

Traditionally women use locust beans to make *daddawa*. The beans are first boiled for at least 24 hours. Water must be added frequently. The cooked beans – still quite firm – are mixed with wood ash and pounded and washed several times to remove the seed coats. The beans are boiled for another three to four hours until they become softer, and are then spread in a large, flat basket, covered with leaves and allowed to ferment for two days. On the third day, the bean mass is transferred to a deep bowl and allowed to ferment for a further 24 hours. It is then spread out again in a large, flat basket and partially dried in the sun for several hours. It is then pounded with a mortar and pestle, before being formed by hand into balls or wafers, which are the finished product. When the *daddawa* is dried thoroughly in the sun, it has very good keeping qualities. The whole production process takes about six days and *daddawa* can be stored in earthenware pots for up to two years.

Innovations in *daddawa* processing

There have been various constraints to an increase in the supply of locust beans, which traditionally are the raw material from which *daddawa* is made. Locust beans are obtained from a leguminous tree, *Parkia clappertonia*, which needs several years to mature, and there are considerable fluctuations in yield from year to year. Furthermore, due to mechanized farming methods, the number of available trees has decreased, while at the same time the demand for *daddawa* has increased.

Nigerian women have overcome these constraints by substituting soybeans for locust beans. In order to keep the qualities of the soybean *daddawa* similar to those of the locust bean product, and to ensure the marketability of the new product, women have had to modify the traditional processing technology.

The new techniques that the women have adopted are more efficient than those in locust bean processing. They fry the soybeans, grind them to remove the skins, then boil them once for about six hours – less than a quarter of the total cooking time required for locust beans. The soybean fermentation process, like that of the locust beans, takes three days. Women see the reduced cooking time and thus the reduced requirement for fuel and water as a big advantage of the adapted processing technique.

Another advantage of using soybeans for *daddawa* is that women can grow their own beans in the fields traditionally allocated for their use, instead of having to buy locust beans or tree harvesting rights. Each locust bean tree is owned by individuals, usually men, who hold the user rights to the plot in which the tree is standing.

Women have integrated soybeans into their traditional cropping systems since it was introduced into Nigeria early this century as a cash crop for export. Small-scale farmers – primarily women – intercrop them with sorghum and/or maize. Nigeria is now the largest producer of soybeans for food in Western and Central Africa, and almost all of the soybean produce in Nigeria is sold, with value added, in the form of *daddawa*. Soybeans have become so accepted by farmers that Abet farm women even refer to their 'traditional' soybean variety as opposed to the new varieties from research institutes and government services. Beans as field crops are traditionally grown by women, but soybean production has become so lucrative that men have also begun to get involved.

Although soybean is an introduced crop, it is important to note that its utilization in the production of local foods was an entirely indigenous innovation, which was stimulated mainly by the unavailability of the traditional raw product and increasing market demand.

Dissemination of women's new technology

In Abet, knowledge about the technology of soybean growing and processing has spread from woman to woman by word of mouth, without any formal groupings, structures or procedures. For instance, women from the Kaje ethnic group, who were among the first ones to substitute soybeans for locust beans, have given neighbouring Fulani women handfuls of seed, encouraged them to try it out in their gardens, advised them about cropping techniques (e.g. timing the harvest before seed-scattering), and showed them how to ferment the beans to make *daddawa* for home consumption. (Waters-Bayer, 1988; Mehratu and Hahn, 1986)

Assmi production in Sri Lanka

A grassroots woman uses her entrepreneurial skills to expand and modify a traditionally household production process.

Assmi is a traditional sweet made of rice flour in Sri Lanka. Although popular at festivals and special events, it was not, until recently, readily available as its production is labour-intensive and highly skilled. However, due to the marketing initiative of Nanda, a Sri Lankan woman entrepreneur, *assmi* is now on sale more widely.

Nanda learned to make *assmi* for local festivities in her home village in rural Sri Lanka. It was only when her husband lost his job, and the family was in need of a new source of income that she started producing the traditional sweet for the market.

The *assmi* production process starts with soaking the rice for about two hours, draining and then pounding it with a mortar and pestle into an extra-fine powder, which is essential for the high quality of the final product. Rice mills cannot be used for this task, as the heat generated slightly cooks the rice and affects the quality of the sweet.

The next stage is the preparation of a sticky paste to be mixed into the rice flour. For this the women use a wild plant, *kale kurundu* in Sinhala and 'jungle cinnamon' in English, the leaves of which exude a sticky, gummy substance when crushed and mixed with water. The runny paste is added to the rice flour and the resulting batter poured into a frying pan through a special perforated spoon.

After frying, the sweets are put aside for three days at room temperature to absorb the natural moisture of the air. This waiting period is crucial, since the structure of the starch molecules changes due to water absorption and a small amount of fermentation, which determines the final quality of the *assmi*. After three days the sweets are fried again. They double in size and the colour changes from beige to milk white, which is an important factor in their marketability.

If Nanda receives an urgent order she puts the sweets in a big bamboo basket which she places outside on the grass overnight so that the morning dew speeds up water absorption by the mixture, and shortens the time before re-frying. She prefers to work inside, however, as animals or insects may contaminate the *assmi* if it is outside.

The final stage is the pouring of a coconut and palm syrup mixture over the *assmi*, which sweetens it and improves the appearance. The women collect the syrup from palm trees in bags made of coconut leaves.

Nanda has been able to apply her innovative skills to the marketing of her product – her husband takes baskets of sweets around the streets by bicycle, selling as he goes. Now she receives orders from big shops in Colombo. Her chances of meeting the increasing demand depend on making the rice pounding process less labour-intensive and time consuming. Purchase of a motorized mortar and pestle is beyond their reach at the moment. At a recently-held science exhibition, a fifteen-year old school girl came up with a very clever design which might provide an answer to Nanda's problem. The young girl's project, which won the second prize, was a mortar and pestle based on magnetism generated by an AC current. Constructing a larger version of this small model might provide a low-cost electrically operated mortar and pestle. (Personal communication – Hidalge, 1991)

Section III
External support to women's technological innovation

Utilization of soybeans in West Africa

Based on the case study in Section II from Nigeria, this example illustrates how external intervention can facilitate the widespread dissemination of an indigenous innovation.

The promotion of the wider application of soybean utilization in West Africa was carried out by the Family Health Advisory Services (FHAS), a Togolese NGO, run by two dynamic West African women, in collaboration with an international NGO. These two organizations facilitated the adaptation of soybeans by rural women in Togo, Ghana, and Mali. The approach used was women-focused, starting from their immediate needs, supporting them in the testing of new ideas, building on initial success, encouraging their participation in overcoming problems, and training women leaders to train their fellow women. 'This approach was based on the capacity of women to learn and to express themselves. It succeeded because of women's dynamic and creative willingness to help other women.' (Gubbels and Iddi, undated)

Research into soybean utilization in Africa by international agricultural research institutions in the early seventies had cited 'poor seed viability, the need for root inoculants for effective nitrogen fixation, and lack of effective markets' as the major constraints upon soybean dissemination in West Africa. The soybean agricultural technology that had already been developed by women, however, challenges

this pessimistic diagnosis. Two local varieties grown by a few individual women scattered throughout the Dapaong district of Northern Togo, and the Nakpanduri area across the border with Ghana, have excellent seed viability, and do not need inoculum to fix nitrogen.

Hence FHAS took up the task of promoting what a few women had learned by themselves in West Africa. The lack of an effective local market for soybeans, which had caused programmes aimed at men to fail, did not affect the efforts of FHAS because of its women-oriented strategy. Soybeans were introduced not as a crop *per se*, but as a type of legume that could be used in making local sauces. This made it of concern only to women, as men generally are not interested in non-commercial crops. The activities relating to women's soybean cultivation and processing and facilitated by FHAS were as follows:

○ *Awareness raising:* women were encouraged to try out the new seed through cooking demonstrations where women prepared local dishes first with local beans and then with soybeans, and evaluated the results themselves; use of visual aids and exchange visits were instrumental – once soybeans were adopted in a few pilot villages, experienced village women went to other villages to demonstrate the new technique.

○ *Setting priorities:* village women decided for themselves how to use the information on the soybean. From the perspective of the project personnel there were many ways in which soybeans could have been used, but it was important that the women chose what they wanted to learn and apply first. Most women chose soybean use in *dad-dawa* making (see previous case study) as a priority.

○ *Testing of new ideas by volunteers:* introducing a new crop is always a risky business since an initial failure can easily discourage other women. Village women were asked to select a few volunteers to try out the soybeans in the first year on behalf of all interested women in the village. The experimenters were provided with regular training and follow-up by project personnel, and then shared their experiences with others.

○ *Training of trainers:* if the test plots produced a good harvest, two volunteer women from each village were invited to a training workshop on soybean preparation techniques, which was hosted by one of the participating villages. This created a feeling of solidarity and a 'home from home' training environment. When the volunteers returned to their villages, they in turn held workshops of their own to train the remaining volunteers who had planted soybeans.

○ *Strengthening of the local technical capacity:* the long-term objective of the project was to strengthen the process whereby women meet together, share information and plan activities. The strengthening of these links or the development or strengthening of institutions was a key component of the activities.

○ *Testing and evaluating new technologies:* women are encouraged to continue the process of testing new ideas on a small scale, and evaluating the results. Enabling women to measure the impact of a new idea is often crucial to its acceptance.

Initially the above techniques were used to facilitate women's adoption of the soybean technology in several pilot villages in Togo, Mali and Ghana. Following the successful adoption of the technology, the soybean would reach a 'take-off' point by developing a local market at which other women bought seeds and started their own production. Women in other villages would also ask for assistance in getting started with soybeans. External intervention based on the above-described strategy would eventually lead to a spontaneous mechanism whereby local women could seek access to technological information and support, and hence generate their own technology. (Gubbels and Iddi, undated)

Soy *mishti* in Bangladesh

This case study shows a local NGO supporting women's production through the utilization of a technical innovation by its women field workers.

Mishti are sweetmeats made from milk solids, which are considered to be foods for entertaining in Bangladesh. While they play an important part in the national diet, the potential for milk substitutes in their production is enormous, particularly in a country like Bangladesh where more than 60,000 tons of milk products were imported in one year (1987–8). Numerous sweetmeat shops operating in Dhaka use thousands of litres of milk every day to produce the *mishti* for the urban market. The partial substitution of soy milk for cow's milk is a way of making valuable milk available for other uses such as children's nutrition, while at the same time reducing the cost of producing sweetmeats and increasing the profits of the many small-scale producers who depend on *mishti* enterprises as their main source of income.

It was the high price of milk, and its limited availability that led Jehanara and Biva Rani Biswas, field workers with the 'Women and Children' Programme of the Bangladeshi NGO called Gono Unnayan Prochesta (GUP) to start preparing sweetmeats with soy milk instead of cow's milk. These two women found, however, that the colour, texture and flavour of the products changed with the new ingredient, and the customers preferred *mishti* made of cow's milk.

Despite the low marketability of this new *mishti* product, Gono Unnayan Prochesta recognized the potential for the idea of soy milk substitution, and supported the development of Jehanara and Biswas' idea further. They found that the different flavour brought about by the soy milk can be camouflaged by using hot water during the grinding of the soy, boiling the milk and adding a little cardamom, and regulating the acidity of the water. The colour problem was partially solved by treating the water with sodium metabisulphate.

Using this technique, darker sweetmeats like *kalajam* and *chamcham* made with 70 per cent soy milk were indistinguishable from those made with cow's milk, even by experienced *karigors* (sweetmakers). Soy milk substitution in the production of white sweetmeats such as *roshagollah* and *shondesh* is currently being tested.

The new products using soy milk have been evaluated twice by sweetmeat producers around Rajoir and, in most cases, they could not tell the difference between the traditional product and the new product.

The producers arranged a market test by selling 10,000 taka-worth of *mishti* in Rajoir and adjacent areas through tea stalls. A group of four women are now producing soy *mishti* for sale through the GUP bakery.

Soy *mishti* production technology has attracted the interest of other national and international NGOs and is being demonstrated in training courses in Bangladesh. (Shamin, 1990)

Mechanical cassava graters in Nigeria

Women's demand for less labour-intensive techniques instigates an innovation by local artisans.

Preparation of *gari* from cassava is a traditional woman's activity in West Africa, and is one of the most popular food-processing industries at household and community levels in the eastern and western parts of Nigeria. The cassava root, when processed into various foods, accounts for 50 per cent of the carbohydrate intake in the country. The processing of cassava into *gari* fulfils two important functions: through this process the concentration of toxins in the raw product is reduced significantly, while its shelf-life, when well-prepared, is extended for up to two years.

Traditional *gari* processing consists of a set of laborious and labour-intensive activities, which has the effect of reducing output levels, creating shortages in the market, raising the price of *gari* beyond the reach of the poor and reducing the income of the majority of women engaged in this activity.

The recent ban on importing food alternatives such as wheat, has led to an increased importance for *gari* in the Nigerian economy, thus providing the motivation for the mechanization of the traditional productive activity. The innovative efforts have concentrated on the cassava grating phase of the processing chain. Traditional grating involved the use of a sheet of perforated metal usually made from the sides of imported kerosene containers. The women would run the peeled casava over the perforated metal sheet until the cassava was reduced to a small lump, which was then discarded. The grater passed through three stages: from completely manual to semi-mechanized to fully mechanized. The changes, some radical, some incremental, came in response to women's search for less laborious techniques, the need to increase *gari* production and the desire by entrepreneurs to sell more graters.

One of the oldest carpenters in Benin is said to have built the first machine in response to his three wives' pleas for more efficient equipment. He used his knowledge of imported cornmills and the information provided by his wives on the processing technique, to modify the manual grater into a longer framed one to enable the women to stand while grating, and shorter framed ones for grating in a sitting position. These two modifications might have come in response to the different specifications that his wives gave him. Later, the same carpenter built a wooden grater that operated on the principle of hand-grating and also a mechanized cornmill. This formed the prototype for the fully mechanized graters that were developed five years later, again by local artisans.

Use of the improved graters diffused rapidly throughout every *gari*-making community. Information about this new technique was passed quickly from one woman to another. If one woman saw it in a neighbourhood she described it to her husband or son who then made one to her specifications. Further suggestions were provided by the women to the local artisans until the right standard of equipment was achieved. The increased demand for *gari* and the hand injuries suffered from manual graters have led to the rapid adoption of mechanized graters.

The semi-mechanized machines of hand-driven or bicycle-driven types were later attempts, mainly by learning and research institutions, to produce equipment at lower cost than that of fully mechanized machines and thus bring the improved technology within the reach of women processors. In contrast to the manual and the fully mechanized graters which were developed in the informal engineering sector and accepted by the women users on a widespread basis, these turned out to be more of a 'technology-push' than a 'demand-pull' innovation. Women rejected the bicycle-driven grater, because bicycles are normally ridden by men, and they gathered that men wanted to establish exclusive operational rights. The hand-driven grater, though estimated to be 50 per cent faster than the traditional model, was considered laborious in operation and its output was inadequate.

Women have been the major instigators of change in the informal engineering sector. In a survey, 78 per cent of the grater producers attributed the changes to women customers' suggestions, while 22 per cent attributed the alterations to the natural quest for improvement in design. Women users of the grater, through their demands, directed changes towards sturdier machines and more durable grating sheets. Interviews carried out with women *gari* processors showed that women felt positive towards technological improvements, particularly as they affect their work. Contrary to prevailing myths, women were very active in providing various suggestions as to how the designs might be improved, based on their rich traditional technical knowledge.

Changes in *gari* processing in Ghana and Sierra Leone

Gari processing technology in Ghana has gone through a similar phase of mechanization. In this case a mechanical grater, a pressing machine to squeeze the water from the grated cassava and a large enamel pan for roasting, which held ten times the volume of the traditional cassava pot, were developed locally with women advising on the design. In response to the increased demand for *gari*, women have obtained funding for men to form a cassava growers' association in order to step up cassava production. (Carr, 1984)

Similar to Ugandan women's adoption of cassava as the raw material in a variety of production processes (see case study in Section II), the worsening economic situation in Sierra Leone has also forced women to use cassava as substitute, in this case for rice, their preferred staple. In Sierra Leone the traditional technology consists of grating by hand using old perforated zinc pans, and then placing heavy stones over the grated cassava in sacks for about one week to squeeze out the water while the product ferments. Most women

processors now recognize that they can shorten the fermentation and watering process by applying even greater pressure. They have pioneered a new method, which involves the pressing of the cassava pulp-filled sack between logs, and tying the logs tightly together to squeeze the pulp. Though it is a simple adaptation, the time gain is significant: this reduces the entire operation to one day. (Adjebeng-Asem, 1990)

Indigenous vegetables in Kenya

Women's experimental activities are supported by both national and international NGOs, in this case for the creation of an environment more conducive to local technical innovation, where women combine 'modern' and indigenous techniques.

Number of indigenous plants named by Mary Owe, aged 23:

Boo
Mito
Akeyo
Apoth
Osuga
Nyasigumba
Odielo
Piupiou
Amondi

Number of indigenous plants named by Sylvia Odero, aged 56:

Piupiou	Dindi	Dek	Osuga
Hariadho	Boo	Boo Dhok	Amondi
Ohinglatiang	Ohulo	Odielo	Anyuongi
Nderm	Onyiego	Nyatiegwen	Achak
Nyathundguogi	Awayo	Angayo	Nyohonyoho
Nyanyiekmon	Achak	Angaya	Nyasigumba
Ong'orang'ora	Apoth	Mandonge	Apoth Matindo
Apoth Machuwa	Apoth Onyulo	Mito	Obudo Nyaduwolo
Adongo Nyayuora	Ododo	Odura	Abuoch
Oruka	Susa	Obuolo	Tigatiga
Nyochengoche	Hwaiga	Ondhondho	Api
Tungu			

Figure 18. Comparison of indigenous knowledge as held by young and old

When Mary Owe, aged 23, of the Okando Women's Group in Utonga, is asked to name all the indigenous vegetables that she knows, she has no problems remembering the first five: 'boo, mito, akeyo, apoth and osuga.' She and the other women of the Utonga sub-location in Kenya's Siaya District prepare these for their families, having either grown or bought the vegetables. Mary has more problems remembering the names of the next four indigenous vegetables she knows from her grandmother: 'nyasigumba, odielo, piupiou, and amondi.' These are among the local delicacies whose usage is rapidly declining due to dietary and socio-economic trends which in recent years have swept through the country. Sylvia Odero, aged 56, of Mary's grandmother's generation, on the other hand, is able to draw up a list of 45 items without much difficulty. Traditionally, the cultivation and marketing of indigenous food plants were carried out mostly by women on a nationwide basis, until the colonial administration insisted that local farmers grow cash crops, mostly exotic species for the international market, rather than subsistence crops, which were dismissed as 'primitive and inferior in quality'.

Advantages of women's use of indigenous plants

'Kenya's food economy is now heavily dependent on wheat and rice. We produce enough of both grains during bumper years, but during lean years we face shortages and are forced to import. Such over-reliance on a few particular foods is dangerous because when a crop fails it is like having a famine. People who have not acquired the knowledge of how to gather, cultivate and make use of indigenous foods become desperate and are often rendered helpless.' So says a nutritionist, in explaining the disadvantages of the exotic species. Unlike the exotics, indigenous plants are disease and drought resistant, are not as prone to major pests, and are less costly to grow since they can do without expensive fertilizers and pesticides. Many also have a nitrogen-fixing capacity. Crop management of indigenous plants is relatively easy and makes fewer demands on women's time and energy. Indigenous crops often grow faster than exotics, and can be harvested in weeks, rather than months. Moreover the preservation of diets rich in indigenous food plants means better nutrition. Indigenous food plants also tend to be environmentally more appropriate.

Low status of indigenous food plants

Women's farming, food processing and marketing in Kenya, as in many other countries, is perceived to be haphazard and small scale. Women who grow indigenous plants, are not credited any value as producers. When a woman is seen cultivating or gathering indigenous food plants, it is assumed that she is doing so because she cannot afford better food. Agricultural policies and extension services often deny the importance of women's knowledge of local food plants by targeting male commercial farmers. Even when women do get involved in agricultural schemes, they have received little support for growing indigenous plants. In one case, one woman farmer in the Siaya District, when asked where she got her indigenous food plants from, pointed outside of her vegetable garden towards the forest. She explained that she had a small plot hidden away there where she planted a few indigenous varieties that she liked to use. As one of the farmers involved in the agricultural extension scheme operational in the area, she was expected to grow only the 'marketable' exotic species, rather than indigenous food crops.

The trend is reversing – women combine indigenous and modern practices

Despite negative opinions about indigenous foods, many rural Kenyan women still believe that indigenous food species are crucial for the livelihood of their families. They communicate as much of their knowledge of indigenous food plants as possible down to the younger generations through informal channels. Recently, some women's groups in the Siaya District have also taken the initiative to grow indigenous vegetables on a commercial basis, and in doing so have upgraded production and processing technologies. For instance, the Okando Women's Group, experimenting to improve production, has proved that indigenous vegetables do well without fertilizer. Instead, women use cattle manure and compost to enrich the soil. Learning from this experience, the group members plan to use the same technologies to grow exotic crops.

Two national NGOs (Kenya Freedom from Hunger Council and Kenya National Museums Council) are now collaborating with an international NGO to support the women in their efforts. They have started a joint programme called the Indigenous Food Plant Programme (IFPP). The implementing agencies maintain that programmes which help to create a positive and encouraging environment for women to make the best of their knowledge of food technologies is the only way to come up with sustainable solutions to the problems of malnutrition and food shortages. The IFPP aims to support women's production, processing and marketing activities of these food plants, as well as document and disseminate information on a widespread basis for the re-introduction and promotion of indigenous food plants in sub-Saharan Africa.

Local names of *Solanum mnavu*

Luo	–	Osuga
Kikiyu	–	Managu
Kamba	–	Kitulu
Meru	–	Mathungu
Rendille	–	Molou
Pokot	–	Ksoiya
Sambura	–	Lekeru
Turkana	–	Esuja
Bukusu	–	Namasaka
Mausai	–	Ormomoi
Kipsigis	–	Isoiyot

Provided by Ogana

Figure 19. The local names of indigenous plants such as the *Solanum mnavu* above, are among the information included in the IFPP species inventory

This support has greatly facilitated women's efforts to upgrade their productive activities and enabled them to make use of modern technologies, where they saw appropriate, to improve their local practices. The council provided the groups with water pumps which they use both for domestic consumption and irrigation. Growing indigenous species by irrigation was unheard of in the past. Traditionally women depended on rain to grow indigenous crops or collected them in the forest. Facing a quite different situation from that which confronted the older generations, where indigenous food plants are now threatened by extinction, women found that with a constant water supply the indigenous vegetables fared better.

Through the extension services provided by IFPP in conjunction with the Ministry of Agriculture, women learn new horticultural management practices. They have started to add their own improvements, such as intercropping local varieties with those from outside sources, which overcomes some of the disadvantages of monocropping (such as vulnerability to disease, weather and soil erosion) and extends the period of time over which women can take different crops to sell at the market.

The group has started collecting seeds of indigenous plants in a move towards self-sufficiency in future. So far, most of their seeds have been provided by the IFPP Programme. Recently they have started collecting, drying and packaging their own indigenous seeds for sale. By increasing their own seed stocks, they hope to retain control and avoid dependence on multinational seed-producing companies, which have begun to take an interest in this potentially lucrative market.

Information dissemination

One of the IFPP programme activities is the preservation of women's knowledge and practices of indigenous food plant species through the documentation and widespread dissemination of this information. The species inventory includes the various local names of the plant, its traditional and present use, methods for gathering and propagating, seasonal aspects, local handling, storage and preparation techniques, nutritional value and other specific properties of the plant. Already the programme has established a database which has over 800 varieties, most of this information being supplied by women. The findings are discussed within academic and scientific circles, and are occasionally disseminated in conferences.

The IFPP therefore aims to channel this information back to the young generations, as well as to the old who are often unaware of its importance. The information is re-packaged into three categories: for schools, adult readers and the general public, which includes local and international NGOs, institutions, government ministries, and individuals. The information material is being developed not only in English, but also in some of the local languages. A network of NGOs involved in similar work is being built through workshops and newsletters. (Ogana, 1991)

Shea butter extraction in Ghana

This case study illustrates participative technology development: where technologists listen to, work together with, and build on the knowledge of women in developing an efficient technology.

Shea butter is widely used in Ghana as the only traditional cooking oil, as well as an ointment and cosmetic. It is also exported to industrialized countries where the butter is used as a substitute for cocoa butter, and in the pharmaceutical and cosmetic industries. The shea nut tree (*Butyrosperum parkii*) grows wild in the savanna of Western and Central Africa in a belt about 5000km long and 600km wide, stretching from Gambia to Southern Sudan. Women in these areas use variations of a traditional extraction technology, which achieves a very high oil extraction rate. In Ghana, women from the Dagomba tribe in the Northern Region are said to have the most advanced traditional technology, which provides an efficiency rate of around 83 per cent to produce shea butter of high quality. The process is nevertheless very time-consuming and labour-intensive. The collection of the shea fruits and their processing into butter is exclusively a woman's job in Northern Ghana and one of the main sources of income for women.

The traditional process

The traditional process of shea butter production involves the following stages: collection of fruits; boiling of fruits to remove the flesh; drying of fruits; deshelling of nuts; drying and storage of kernels; crushing of kernels; roasting of crushed kernels; grinding of paste; kneading of paste and creaming; clarification and crystallization. Kneading is the most crucial step in determining the quality of

Savannah belt

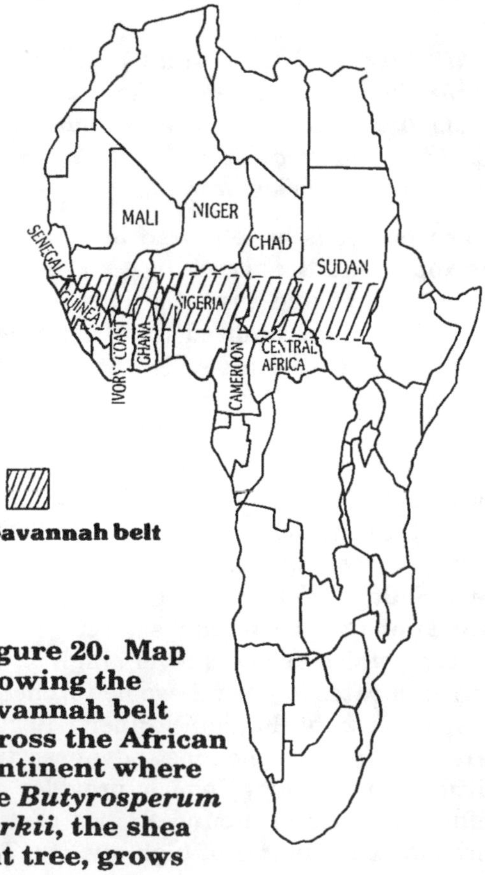

Figure 20. Map showing the savannah belt across the African continent where the *Butyrosperum parkii*, the shea nut tree, grows

the final product. Its successful execution depends on the recognition of changes in appearance, colour, viscosity and temperature of the kneaded mass, possible only for the well-trained and experienced eye to see.

In the clarification and crystallization phase, the washed cream is heated in a big pot. The clear oil that is formed is collected with a ladle into a smaller pot. Scum floating on top of the oil is discarded. The clarified oil is poured into clean, enamelled basins and left to cool overnight. In the morning the oil starts to crystallize, sometimes after 'seeding' with a small lump of shea butter from a previous batch. The mass is stirred at hourly intervals with a wooden spoon until the oil has been transformed into a semi-cold state. The shea butter is then transferred into the semi-spherical bottom part of a calabash and built up to a round, yellowish-white lump. This is covered with a piece of cloth and stored until it is taken to the market.

Modifications to the traditional processing technology

The first attempt at the mechanization of the shea butter production process came from the women themselves. They adapted the corn mill, which was introduced to Ghana 32 years ago at the time of independence, for the grinding of roasted shea nut granules. The crushing, removing of kernels and kneading activities were still done by hand. The second attempt, supported by the National Council of Women in Development (NCWD), was the introduction of the Mali oil extractor to the Dagomba women who abandoned it after a few trials. They felt that this extractor did not give them as much oil as the traditional method, and the quality of the final product was poor.

The NCWD, this time together with two international development agencies,

Shea nuts are an important source of food and income for many women

This mechanized kneading machine has been modified on the basis of the women's requirements and knowledge

Dagomba women selling shea butter at the local market

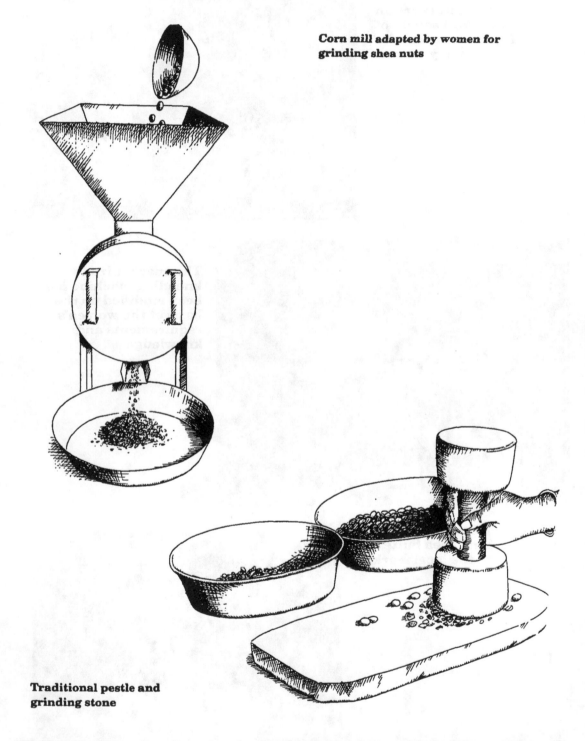

Corn mill adapted by women for
grinding shea nuts

Traditional pestle and
grinding stone

Figure 21. Manual and mechanized technologies for crushing of shea nut kernels

intervened using a different approach. This time, instead of attempting to import a machine designed elsewhere, like the Mali oil extractor, they employed a local engineering enterprise to produce machines to substitute the traditional manual processes. Machines to mill, crack and crush the nuts were developed and proved acceptable, but the kneader was abandoned by most women after a few trials. The women were not consulted over the design of these machines.

Technology development: women and technologists work together

The next attempt to produce a kneading machine was based on full co-operation with the women shea butter producers. The extension workers from a local technology centre acted as communicators between the engineers and the women producers. The project team initially studied in depth the traditional method of production, particularly the kneading stage, in the village. Initial trials with the women shea butter producers have shown that the traditional extraction method has an efficiency of around 83 per cent which compares favourably with present day industrial technology. This convinced the project team further that the traditional technology which the women had developed over centuries through trial and error was an efficient one that produced high quality butter. Further improvements were needed to make the process less time- and energy-consuming for women.

The traditional method of kneading involves dipping the hand into the paste and stirring vigorously. While stirring with the hand, women can tell what to do next by the temperature and feel of the mass on their hand. When the paste is thick and difficult to stir, hot water needs to be added. When the paste is slippery, it means that the fat is melting, so cold

water needs to be added. The addition of hot or cold water at particular times is an important component of the production process, which determines the quality of the final product and the efficiency of the extraction rate.

When the project staff had gone into the village and worked with the women, they learned that the first mechanized kneader had been rejected because it simply stirred rather than kneaded. Acting as communicators between the women producers and the technologists, the project staff recommended the contracted engineer to design a more efficient baffle-impeller arrangement in the kneader along the guidelines provided by the women.

The best results obtained from the nine trials to establish the best possible performance of the kneader gave an extraction rate slightly lower than the manual process, but a reduction of about 66 per cent in the working time. There are still some shortcomings of the mechanical kneader, but the established dialogue between the women and the designers, where the latter are instructed by the former, is expected to lead eventually to an acceptable kneader.

Two technologists with different attitudes, two rates of success

Throughout the course of several attempts at the mechanization of shea butter production under different schemes, the producers in pilot villages have been exposed to different technologists using different methodologies, and achieving different rates of success with oil extraction. Women producers in one of the pilot villages tell the following story to illustrate how the attitude of an outsider can make all the difference in women's willingness to co-operate, and consequently the success of the project:

First, the technologist from town X arrived to study our traditional method of shea butter production and explore the potential for achieving better efficiency rates. As we were going through the various stages, he would time the processes such as kneading, when to add water, and so on, look at his watch, tell us to stop, or to continue on without listening to whether we thought it was the right time to do these things. The few times we tried to express our opinions, he would not hear them. So eventually, we just gave up, and got on with what he instructed us to do just for his own satisfaction. We knew that the amount of oil extracted at the end was going to be low because he was making us do all sorts of wrong things.

After a few months, a second technologist came into the village. The way he worked with us was very different from the first one. At every stage of production, he would enquire why we were doing things the way we were, and really listen. Once we felt that he had an ear to lend us, we started listening to him as well. Eventually we got a much larger amount of oil from that trial. So if you want to get our message across to the people who are involved in such work, it is simple: just tell them to listen!' (Wallace-Bruce, 1991)

Women's milk production in the Bolivian Andes

Women in the Andes illustrate that innovation in the organization of production is as important as a change of equipment.

Dairy farming in the Andes is characterized by poor soils that are suitable only for annual crops, a cold climate, little irrigation and disputes over property ownership. Milk production is therefore low as lack of investment has constrained the development of improved techniques which could potentially augment women's meagre incomes. The women themselves have limited access to education, have tended to be overlooked in technology transfer programmes, and exercise little power as individuals in their transactions with the industrial milk buyers.

SETAM (Technical Services for Women), a local NGO, identified some of the more pressing local problems facing women. While many of these derived from the socio-economic conditions common in many rural societies such as pressure on land, lack of basic infrastructural services, subsistence economies, forced migration and little technical investment, others related directly to the low status of women and exploitation of their agricultural production.

On the basis of discussions with women, SETAM identified four elements to the programme, based on the women's skills and priorities. These were:

o organization of the women milk producers;
o improvement in the care of cattle;
o milk production; and
o re-evaluation of women's productive role.

The inter-relationship between these factors means that results cannot only be measured in quantitative terms, such as the increase in milk production, but also in terms of the personal development of the beneficiaries.

In this case what has turned out to be the most important result is the organization of women milk producers, which has enabled them to oppose the exploitation of their milk production. With the support of SETAM, the women got together to create an association of milk producers, comprising eight smaller, already existing associations. This organization has given the women power to negotiate higher prices for their product with the state-owned industrial milk plant (PIL), which had previously dealt with the women milk producers on an individual basis. The strength of the organization has given the women a higher status, and has enabled them to achieve a new identity as producers, which has in turn improved the communities' and the women's own view of milk production.

Through working with the milk producers' organization the women have widened their circle of contacts and have used the meetings to deal with other problems in their lives. They claim that the improved social interaction has enabled them to have the confidence to speak out, and that they have improved their skills to think and to analyse.

Milk production in the area has also increased. The producers have received training, in their own language, which has enabled them to build on their knowledge of cattle care and milk production. The area is producing around 1000 litres per day, which means that the family of each milk producer now receives an amount equivalent to a basic salary. 'Now I feel much more secure, economically,' claimed one woman. (Yara Carafa, 1991)

Livestock production in Peru

Women's technological innovation is promoted and facilitated by a local NGO. The case study highlights some of the lessons to be learned by project staff in facilitating women's involvement in technology development.

The Small Ruminant Collaborative Research Programme Project in Peru is a participatory research initiative with women farmers. This project was launched by Grupo Yanapai, a non-profit research organization, in collaboration with the Peruvian National Institute for Agricultural Research and Extension. In the communities in which the project team worked, crop and livestock production are closely linked. Livestock production, seed selection, care and planting, and food processing are completely performed by women, while harvesting and cultivation work is shared with men.

The aim of the project was to support peasant farmers' own research and experimentation for improving the crop and livestock production system in highland Peru. This was based on the recognition that food production and processing activities and any technological improvements in this area cannot be separated from the rest of people's lives. Hence the best change could be brought about only by the people themselves.

Initially the community assemblies appointed a committee for each community which would collaborate in the planning, implementation and evaluation of experiments on production problems. Although there was no gender restriction on the committee membership, and despite the project team's request that women be included, the communities named only men.

The project team started working with these committees of men in weekly meetings. In the initial phase of problem identification and planning, the suggestions were only on crop production. The project team kept suggesting that similar experiments be conducted on livestock production as well, until the men finally told the team 'Please, stop talking to us about animals, we don't have anything to do with animals. The people who really manage and produce animals are the women. If you people want to talk about animals, you'd better talk with the women.' Because of the way the assembly was organized, the project team had regarded the men as heads of the households in the community and therefore as specialists in all aspects of the farming system, including animal husbandry.

The men's suggestion was brought before the community assembly which resulted in the appointment of women to the collaborating committees. In subsequent meetings, however, it became apparent that the women did not feel comfortable in the committee, and the team was still unable to work systematically on animal production. Women's lack of experience in active group discussion and their lower level of education made them feel shy before those (men) more formally educated. In an effort to overcome this limitation, the project team called the women informally with a proposal to work on production problems which were of importance to them. Within a month about one-third of the women were participating in weekly meetings. The formation of separate women's groups discussing the productive areas of most interest to them, such as grazing and animal health care, helped to facilitate women's experimentation. The women very clearly identified parasite control, provision of supplementary animal fodder, improvement of natural pasture quality, seed selection and storage, and adequate planting densities as their priority problems, and willingly started working on them with the support of the project staff.

The differences in 'scientific' languages

When the problem of internal parasites in sheep was discussed in the weekly meetings, women cited a high incidence of liver-fluke in sheep. They expressed the belief that this illness was caused by the ingestion of a small leaf found in marshy areas or at the edge of streams. For this reason, when possible, they kept the cattle away from these areas where the leaf was found. Upon research along the guidelines provided by the women, the project team identified that it was the cysts which later developed into parasites, that were found on the leaves of

vegetation in humid places, that caused the illness, rather than the leaves themselves. The team decided to include a talk on the liver-fluke cycle in the programmed community information series.

The talk was prepared by a research professor, with complementary graphics, and programmed consecutively in three participating communities. During these sessions, which were attended by groups of between 50 and 100 men, women and children, it became evident that although the researcher had taken great care to make the presentation in simple Spanish, his audiences had problems relating to both the talk and the graphics. One example of this was people's surprise when specimens of snails (which are hosts to the parasite during one stage of its life cycle) were passed round at the end of the meeting. The graphics had led them to believe that the actual size of the snails was about ten times larger!

Before the second session, with help from the community collaborators and the project team, an effort was made to identify the local vocabulary used to designate relevant plants, animals and insects in order to facilitate a clearer communication of the problem. The specimens were passed round both before and after the talk, and comparisons made between the real-life specimens and the graphics. During the second talk it was immediately evident from the interest shown and the questions asked that much more was being understood.

While the scientists attempted to explain facts about organisms not visible to the naked eye, the village men and women utilized distinct visual and verbal codes, which the scientists found it difficult to understand. Both languages are 'scientific' in their own right, and the villagers' way of explaining things is no less technically sound than the scientists' way. The women's knowledge of livestock diseases is based on considerable, time-tested, empirically accurate information. In some Quechua highland communities, using this knowledge, local agropastoralists have even been known to incorporate many Western-world items into their veterinary therapies, like using old battery acid or burnt motor oil in combination with other traditional materials and magic/religious practices to treat their herd animals (McCorkle, 1989).

Despite the extensive nature of women's knowledge of livestock production, however, it is by no means complete. Women, lacking microscopes, chemical reagents, access to research and so forth are understandably ignorant of the role of many agents of disease that are invisible to the human eye or that are linked to animal diseases through complex, indirect, parasitic life cycles. Their acquisition of such knowledge can be of crucial value in helping them to take effective steps towards fighting against many of the illnesses that plague their herds. However, as the above example shows, even in situations where there is mutual openness to exchange between researchers, exchange agents and the local people, the difference of languages and communication methods may cause misunderstandings and a lack of confidence on both sides.

Participatory research with local people

The project team found that it was most successful at working with local people over problem definition, trial implementation and analysis of results, but that it needed to improve its techniques to encourage more participation in designing the research phase. The team had difficulty in explaining basic concepts in the trials, and a majority of the prototypes had to be patched up after observing that they were not working out as originally designed.

The team identified the following measures as necessary for development workers when working together with local people in technology development:

o willingness to take part in a mutual learning process with the community so as to be able to adapt new methods to the local production systems, taking ecological, economic and social organizational factors into account;

o simple and specific research plans which permit rapid modification or adjustment to new findings, as well as to unforeseen climatological and organizational factors;

o communication with the local people in a comprehensible language, and exchange of technical information using local terminology.

All these requirements put new demands on the development practitioner and suggested a new method of technology development, one that is based on a real dialogue with the local people. *Working together with* rather than *for* local people in a participatory way would eventually lead to the generation of information, technology and knowledge which would translate into action. In other words, the additional time put into breaking down the communication barriers would be compensated by less time being required between the generation and adoption of technology. Local people would stand to gain more control over the technology development and technical change process, and their dependence on outside intervention would decrease. (Fernandez, 1988)

Women squash producers in Zaire

Women's local capacity to experiment, analyse and innovate is supported by pro-

ject staff and a participatory extension approach is developed.

This pilot project, which was conducted jointly by an international women's organization and a local technology centre – the Centre Agricole Lusekele – with the aim to reach women farmers in four collectives in Bulungu Zone, Central Bandundu, Zaire illustrates how technology development by grassroots women producers can be facilitated by a participatory approach.

Women farmers in Bandundu had traditionally adapted and used a variety of food cycle technologies. The significance of the project lies in its recognition of women's informal innovative activities, and the participatory methodology by which external support was provided to fill gaps which women themselves had identified in their existing networks of production.

The context of women's production in Bandundu

Agriculture is a major source of income for over 90 per cent of the women in the Bandundu area, where adult male participation in agriculture is the lowest in the country. Women farmers here produce food not only for household and village consumption, but also for urban centres such as Kinshasa and Kikwit. It also provides revenue for household expenses, in many cases greater than that produced by male labour. Despite its critical importance, women's farm production is characterized by very low returns on labour which is primarily due to women's lack of control over productive resources. Although women have almost total responsibility for food production, they have little control over the land they farm and very limited access to extension services and to labour.

The time that women have available to work in their fields is limited by a number of external factors. Women are responsible for virtually all domestic chores, such as processing and preparation of food, and caring for the children and the sick. They also carry out unpaid labour for the state. Women and men are supposed to participate in *salongo* (community labour) together, but as women are more accessible and easily controlled, it is their labour that is more often called upon for the clearing of forested areas or participation in the state building schemes. Women also participate in parish work and other development activities such as village health committees. Most women are able to draw on family labour for specific tasks, but not on a regular basis.

In addition to a shortage of labour, ecological factors such as declining soil fertility, a higher incidence of plant disease and the spread of strangling weeds are other constraints to women's food production. The economic crisis stemming from the collapse of the palm oil companies and weak investment in rural areas means very uneven commercialization of women's crops and the disappearance of farm opportunities for women. Outmigration and an increased squeeze on small producers from financially pressed local authorities differentially affect women because women lack a power-base within the village or government.

Women's farming and food processing tools are simple and few. The tools are usually made locally but are difficult to obtain. For food processing and preparation and carrying water, women themselves make baskets, gourds and a great range of household utensils. No fertilizers or pesticides are available to the farmers in the area. Women carry all products from the field to home or the market on their heads. Animal traction is never used, indeed some men say that they would not want to tire out the cattle by lending them to the women to carry items.

Adaptations in farming techniques in response to harsh conditions

In adapting to the harsh conditions of production, the Bandundu women have had to change their farming techniques, in some cases choosing to use less sophisticated techniques and to produce less in order to solve their most important problem: shortage of labour.

Most women farmers decided to drop labour-intensive techniques such as mounding, weeding twice and tilling the soil before planting. Instead they started using less labour-intensive techniques to increase soil fertility, such as cutting, burning and leaving fields fallow. Some women use a savanna technique uncommon in the area, which they learned and adapted from women in the Bagata Zone: they cut vegetation, let it rot in the field and then plant seed beds to increase soil fertility. Ridging and mounding, two techniques used commonly in the past, are not popular any more because women do not have enough time to do it, although they know that it increases soil fertility. Another technique, which was suggested to the women by the project staff, was to remove the roots while tilling the soil for peanuts. However, after initial trials, women have dropped it because they did not find it increased yields sufficiently to justify labour time. Monocropping is another farming technique that women are moving away from in response to diminished time available for farming. While in the past each crop had its own field (which might possibly be linked to the rotations introduced in the past under the Belgian compulsory cropping system), now women plant crops in association. Some of the labour intensive varieties of food crops have also been dropped and replaced by crops that require less time and fewer inputs to grow.

Innovations by women under the project scheme

The two-women project team, which consisted of an expatriate agricultural extension specialist and a Zairian rural development technician from the local technology centre, supported local women in the analysis of their own technical problems and the search for solutions to low agricultural production. The project team did not impose on the local producers what they thought were the best solutions, but instead facilitated women's own experimentation through on-farm trials, provision of technical advice, and exchange visits which enabled the sharing of technological information with women farmers from other areas.

One of the successful examples of technical change carried out by the women farmers participating in the project was in squash production. Squash is a key women's crop in the area, for household consumption as well as for sale. Nevertheless, research and extension advice on squash is virtually non-existent, since it is strictly in the domain of women's farming and therefore not perceived to be important.

An exchange visit provided the main impetus for the innovation in this case. The women farmers in Lusekele, the project area, have traditionally farmed forest land. In recent years, however, the Lusekele area has undergone rapid deforestation, turning it into a savanna area. Lusekele women's lack of knowledge of appropriate techniques for poorer savanna soils has led to decreasing yields. During one of the regular informal meetings with the project team, some women mentioned the successful squash harvest of the farmers in the Idiofa Zone, which had always been a savanna area. A field trip was organized to Idiofa to facilitate an exchange of information between Idiofa women who were experts on savanna farming and the Lusekele women who were new to savannah farming. Although the exchange was set up to deal with squash and millet, women also exchanged information on soil conservation and intercropping with leguminous trees.

Upon return from this exchange visit, women chose to plant fields of squash and millet using methods that they learned in Idiofa, with some minor modifications. The trial application of these adopted techniques has worked successfully, and women in Lusekele are starting to apply these techniques on a wider basis.

The reasons for the project's success

An overwhelming majority of the women farmers are continuing to work and consult with the project team with increasing enthusiasm. Most women state that they find the support of the project extension workers useful. The team attributes the success of their collaboration with the women to the following participatory techniques.

1. *The planning, action and evaluation cycle was based around problems and solutions women had identified:* there was no pre-designed workplan. From the very beginning, project activities were planned, implemented and evaluated by the women with facilitation from the project extension workers. Although initially this was difficult, after a time women took over the ownership of the initiative so much that they were calling meetings on their own and the project team was informed of those meetings which had taken place in their absence.

2. *Working in groups:* groups proved a safer and a more conducive environment for women to express their opinions and exchange information. One of the women says: 'Each one of us has knowledge, but not all the knowledge. We added up our knowledge and now, due to the group,

some of our problems are gone. We had many problems before.'

3. *Appropriate leaders were allowed to emerge from the group:* group leaders were not appointed. In time individuals who were seen as the representatives of the whole group eventually gained prominence by themselves.

4. *Community fields were used for trials and experimentation:* women decided which, and also what size and shape of field to use for experimentation.

5. *The project extension team neither withheld information, nor controlled the discussion:* this required a real balancing between the tendency of the outsiders to offer and impose solutions on one hand, and no sharing of technical expertise with the women on the other hand. One of the project team members describes the dilemma as follows: 'Theoretically, you say, "Oh yes, women know what they are talking about." Then you get out there and the immediate tendency as a "professional" and a so-called "expert" is to tell them what to do. You catch yourself offering your own solutions to their problems. Then you pull yourself back for the women to find the solution completely on their own, while there are truly useful things that you might have to offer. Only you have to know what kind of support and how. It is a delicate balance.'

6. *Facilitate information transfer among producers of different expertise:* exchange of information between the different villages, areas, as well as different individual producers within the same village can be very conducive to innovative solutions. This can be done through group discussions, exchange visits, etc.

7. *Low risk interventions:* small-scale, subsistence level producers cannot afford to take risks, and hence will prefer solutions which imply less time, labour and financial inputs – proposed solutions should take account of this. (Russel and Requena, 1990; Reid at AWID Conference, 1991)

4

Lessons learned from the case studies

WHILE THE CASE STUDIES in Chapter 3 look at a variety of food cycle technologies that women use in different parts of the world, at different levels of technical sophistication, some common issues and lessons emerge relating to women's local knowledge, innovation and their roles in technology development. These issues and lessons, discussed below, require careful consideration in the planning and implementation of technical assistance programmes concerned with food production, processing and marketing by women.

1. Women's technological innovation does not only involve hardware, because technology is not only hardware. It is the skills, expertise, techniques and organization, in fact the whole body of knowledge, connected with a production process, which women adapt, change and improve according to their priorities.

Many food cycle technologies which women use consist of a series of processes, the major component of which is knowledge. These processes fulfil an important function, but require little hardware other than equipment such as gourds in which to process milk, or a knife to cut fruit for drying. In many cases, the equipment is made by the women themselves using materials readily available in their environment. In the case of water purification in Sudan, for instance, the technology is simple: the crushed *moringa oleifera* seeds are mixed with water in a calabash container; but the knowledge behind the process provides a product of vital importance: clean drinking water. Smoking a gourd to slow down the spoil-

ing of milk is another women's technology in Sudan and Kenya which does not use any hardware, but fulfils an important function of community livelihood.

In many cases, the most important component of women's technology is expertise and skills based on years of trial-and-error experience. The crucial factor in the production of high quality salt in Sierra Leone, for instance, is the skill involved in the evaporation of water, where incorrect observation and an untimely decision to continue boiling can ruin the whole batch. Similarly, Quechuan women's knowledge of plant breeding and biodiversity is what constitutes the potato production technology in the Andes; it involves no hardware at all, just extremely specialized knowledge built up over years.

For Bolivian women milk producers, exploitation was a major problem. Their reorganization as a group, which enabled them to stand up to the industrial milk buyers, improved both their incomes and their status. Such changes in the organization of production are also technical innovations, but do not necessarily involve changes to the hardware.

Marketing can be an integral part of the technology development process – the entrepreneurial initiative of a woman producer of *assmi* in Sri Lanka constituted the main imperative for changes in the traditional production techniques. The focus on hardware in mainstream technology development often leads to undermining the 'software', such as the skills involved and the knowledge in carrying out intricate processes and the organization of production.

Where more straightforward hardware is used, women may be either directly involved in the design and construction, such as the *lutsaga* (storage unit) in Kenya or the salt filtration funnels in Sierra Leone, or indirectly involved in the design and development, as with the shea butter extractor in Ghana and the mechanized roller drier in Sudan. In both cases, women's knowledge of production processes and product quality plays an essential role in the design of the machinery. However, as illustrated by both cases, the mechanized hardware, despite its advantages of labour and time-saving, may produce less popular products than women's unmechanized technologies. Both the homemade *kissra* bread in Sudan and the shea butter produced by women in Ghana using a grinding stone and mortar and pestle were preferred by the consumers over the new products.

2. Women's knowledge of production processes, although scientifically based, remains largely invisible. Nevertheless women constantly use their knowledge to make rational economic and technical choices and changes appropriate to their environment.

Women's activities at the grassroots level are often unrecognized or undervalued by policymakers and development practitioners. Hence the technical knowledge and skills that they have are either ignored or regarded as being of low status, and hence undermined in the design and implementation of food technology policies and programmes. Examples of this invisibility include national and international programmes in Uganda which encouraged the introduction of Nile perch to Lake Victoria with no consideration of women's use of the *nkejje* fish; the promotion of exogenous crops in Kenya, initially by the colonial administration and later by formal extension services, to the extent

of making the use of indigenous plants almost non-existent; the promotion of wheat in Sudan where women traditionally use sorghum; and in Ghana, the technologist who did not hear the suggestions of the women in shea butter extraction trials.

Despite its undermining by policymakers and development practitioners, women's knowledge is scientifically based. In Sudan women carry out 40-step fermentation processes with utmost care. This allows foods to be preserved for up to two years despite the hot climate. Each step has a biochemical explanation. Women know how to use and treat enzymes as they would be used and treated in a laboratory. Women who live hundreds of miles apart in this area, with no apparent communication channels between them, perform identical technical steps with the same precision. In Zimbabwe, women use their knowledge of alkaline and acidic properties in the processing and use of indigenous wild plants. In Kenya, women potters utilize their knowledge of the properties of different clay sources and proportions of mixtures in making durable pottery products and fuel-efficient stoves. Women salt extractors in Sierra Leone possess knowledge about the intricate chemical processes of salt solubility and crystallization rates of sodium chloride *vis-a-vis* other salts.

In order to appreciate the scientific nature of women's knowledge it has to be accepted that grassroots women have their own experimental methods, understanding and language, which may be different from those of professionals trained in formal science and technology institutions. Women processing *jak* and breadfruit in Sri Lanka, for instance, use the 'finger nail' test before terminating blanching. This test is critical in determining the final quality of the product. Colour, feel, consistency, temperature and taste, are all means through which women test, experiment and explain.

Women use their knowledge to make rational technical and economic decisions. Women in Uganda, for instance, choose the traditional *nkejje* fish over the Nile perch and, to the superficial observer, this is a matter of traditional culture according value to the *nkejje*. This tradition, in turn, is based on the local people's observations through time, of the effectiveness of *nkejje* in combating malnutrition and childhood ailments. The *daddawa* producers in Nigeria knew that there was a viable market for their product and reasoned that they could adapt their skills to use soybeans instead of locust beans. Women shea butter producers in Ghana made a technical decision in adopting the mechanized crusher. They rejected the kneading machine, and continued to use their traditional technology because they did not find the quality of the new product acceptable to consumer demands. Sudanese women choose to use the newly introduced technology of alum as a water coagulant only for washing water, since they believe that alum-treated water causes gastro-intestinal disturbances and abortions during pregnancies. For drinking water they continue to use the traditional method of the moringa seeds.

The 'invisibility' of women's knowledge becomes more worrying when possible solutions to serious crises are not explored. Women in Sudan have many techniques for preserving traditional foods to carry them through times of drought and food shortage, and yet drought relief in Sudan is based on foods that are surplus to requirements in countries of the North, not on local skills and experience in the South.

3. Women's knowledge and skills in food production, processing and marketing play a crucial role in household livelihood and food security. The role that women's technological knowledge and skills play in these areas is an issue identified in all the case studies.

Some of the clearest examples are: innovation of cassava processing techniques by Ugandan women after the civil war which wiped out all other crops; Tonga women's adaptations and modifications of their traditional knowledge of indigenous foodstuffs to cope with food shortages in Binga; traditional storage techniques, like the *lutsaga*, helping to preserve the produce in Kenya where a substantial portion of crop yield is wasted each year due to lack of storage facilities; fruit preservation by poor women in Sri Lanka as a means of providing food for the off-season or rainy days when roads and shops are inaccessible; women in Sierra Leone using salt marketing as a major cash income source during the dry season when they wait for agricultural activity to start again; and Ugandan women's utilization of the *nkejje* fish in fighting malnutrition.

There is a surprising lack of focus on gender and indigenous resources in food security programmes, despite women's extensive role in food security in most countries. In Sudan, for example, where there are periodic droughts and famine, the women have already developed many appropriate fermentation techniques to preserve and enrich foodstuffs. With some external support, such techniques have the potential to improve food supplies throughout the year, even in times of drought and food scarcity. A Sudanese engineer explains it thus: 'What we need is not Dutch butter and Danish cheese in food aid packages, but support to the producers of food in this nation, who are predominantly women.'

4. Women's indigenous knowledge and skills are not static. Women mod-

ify, adapt or change production processes in response to various factors, such as national disasters, environmental changes, market demands, conflicts and many more. However small these changes may be, they are innovations.

Grassroots women, despite limited resources, are technically capable of responding to changing conditions of production, and developing innovative solutions to problems. Sometimes the more drastic the changes and the worse their access to resources, the more innovative their solutions seem to be. The Tonga tribe's involuntary move to a poorer agro-ecological zone led women to start gathering, cultivating, processing and utilizing wild plants, which people in other parts of the country cannot even identify.

Similarly, in Uganda, after years of civil war, women made use of the only available raw material, cassava, in every possible way, from food and drink, to building material, medicine, glue and starch – not only for household consumption but also to sell.

A decrease in food supply seems to be a major factor in instigating local technological innovations by women. To make the diminishing supplies of *nkejje* fish last longer, women in Jinja, Uganda, started to dry and pound the fish into a powder, a product which is now commonly found in supermarkets in the area. The substitution of soy beans for locust beans in *daddawa* production in Nigeria, or soy milk for cow's milk in *mishti* production in Bangladesh are all responses by women to decreasing supplies of raw produce. In each case women draw on their knowledge to adapt processing techniques so as to ensure the high quality and marketability of the end product.

Women's traditional technologies also constitute 'historical' examples of innovation, considering the factors that led to their initial development. Dirar, the author of the Sudanese case studies, suggests, for example, that the original development of complicated fermentation techniques by Sudanese women may have been prompted by two factors. First, the adoption of Islam by the Sudanese, which necessitated long pilgrimages to Mecca and required lightweight, easy-to-prepare, preserved foodstuffs for those journeys. Second, the periodic droughts and famine to which Sudan is subject may have encouraged women to experiment with methods of transforming readily available products in their environment into food. Women sometimes respond by organizing productive activities differently. Women potters in Kenya, for example, have started firing pots together in order to overcome a shortage of fuelwood, and Bolivian women milk producers have responded to an exploitative situation by organizing themselves as a group.

Under certain circumstances, women may also make technical changes which decrease their productivity. In response to labour and time constraints, women farmers in Zaire have started to adopt less labour-intensive farming techniques, which in terms of increasing soil fertility are less effective. Nevertheless, these techniques have enabled the women to continue to produce crops despite increasing labour shortages.

In less difficult circumstances, other factors may stimulate innovation, such as women's perception of market potential or the search for less laborious and more productive techniques. The woman *assmi* producer in Sri Lanka, for instance, developed her home-based enterprise as she perceived the market potential for this traditional sweetmeat. Similarly, the Luo women potters in Kenya innovated product design, making new products in response to the loss of markets for traditional pots. Women salt extractors in Sierra Leone, on the other hand, developed the salt-from-silt technique which saved them from walking long distances to the sea and conserved scarce firewood. The case study from Sri Lanka illustrates how women adapt processes on a daily basis to cope with changes in the weather, as well as taking into account the availability of time and labour.

Women also adapt newly-introduced technology to their specific uses, when they find it appropriate. In Ghana they have adapted the corn mill for grinding the shea nuts, while in Sierra Leone women have adapted a traditional technology used in soap making (perforated baskets) to salt extraction.

5. Innovations by women are based on their perception of risks which relate to all aspects of their lives.

The risk factor plays an important role in shaping technology development by women. Women's decisions to reject particular technologies, or not to grow particular crops, are often dismissed as a sign of 'being resistant to change' or 'conservative'. Usually, however, such decisions are valid, based as they are on women's extensive knowledge of their environments, their resources, their own priorities and the risks that they can afford to take.

For example, women salt extractors in Sierra Leone rejected the improved fuel-efficient two-burner chimney stoves, because their maintenance required a blacksmith, which meant their repairs could cost a whole season's income for the producer. The Tonga women in Zimbabwe and similarly the Luo, the Kikuyu and other women in Kenya, continue to cultivate indigenous crops around their gardens, despite extension advice to the contrary, because they do not want to be dependent on exotic crops which run a high risk of failure under unfavourable climatic cir-

cumstances. Women's ability to balance the risks of a newly-introduced technology, as the *daddawa* example from Nigeria shows, may involve linking a new product (soybeans) with a traditional one (*daddawa*) in an innovative way.

6. The informal communication channels for the transfer of technical information and skills between women play an important role in the survival of technical knowledge through generations. External agents must appreciate indigenous means of communication in order to communicate effectively with local women.

Survival of women's technological knowledge and skills is made possible through informal means of information sharing and training. For instance, food sharing and food exchange, a common practice among the rural Sri Lankan communities, is a means of information transfer about new processing methods.

Luo women potters, similarly, share their knowledge of clay sources and transfer skills not only between the generations in the same locality, but also across different geographic areas through marriage. This also applies to shea butter producers in Ghana and salt extractors in Sierra Leone. In the case of fermentation techniques in Sudan, historical evidence shows that as women travelled they shared their skills across the continent all the way to West Africa.

Informal communication systems play an important role in the survival of traditional information, and acquire more importance as circumstances change. It was due to the older generations passing on their technical knowledge that younger women in Zimbabwe and Kenya were able to further develop their use of indigenous plants when faced with food shortages.

The comparison from Kenya of the different amounts of information about indigenous plants held by a 23-year-old woman and by her grandmother's generation, and the example of potato breeders in Peru, both clearly demonstrate that important traditional information is being lost. There is need for support for the documentation and widespread dissemination of such information, similar to that being carried out in Kenya with indigenous plants. There is also a need for South-South exchanges of technological knowledge and skills. At a seminar on 'Women and Technological Innovation in Asia', which was held in Bangladesh, the paper on *jak* preservation in Sri Lanka stimulated many questions from a curious Bangladeshi audience, who were familiar with the consumption of the fresh fruit, but had never heard of its use in processed form.

Similarly, Ugandan women have learned some of the cassava-processing techniques through exchange visits to Ghana, and there is potential for exchanges of information on the uses of tamarind between Zimbabwe, where the fruit is available but under-utilized, and other countries where the fruit is used in many different ways.

Outsiders need to consider the ways in which information is shared within and between communities, and also the form in which information is presented, as the Peru livestock example illustrates: scientists were able to share technical information with local people more effectively when they modified their terminology, approach and thinking.

The story of the two technologists working with women shea butter extractors in Ghana shows that communication between outsiders and local women has to be based on understanding of and respect for local production systems. The more the outsiders are ready to listen to and work 'with' rather than 'for' women, the better will be the communication, and hence the more effective and useful their input and support.

7. Technology development based on indigenous knowledge and innovation has many advantages.

Technologies based on local knowledge, skills and practices:

o usually make best use of the local resources: indigenous vegetables which need less water in Kenya and Zimbabwe; utilization of all parts of the cassava plant in Uganda to meet all kinds of basic needs, from food to building materials;

o respond better to users' priorities: *nkejje* fish in Uganda which supplied a nutritional supplement for children; *daddawa* production from soybeans, which provided a required seasoning and income for the women; dried, fermented foods in Sudan, as a hedge against food shortages;

o are low cost: the *Moringa oleifera* seeds as water coagulants in Sudan, the use of smoke as a preservative in various countries; and tamarind as a supplement to staple foods in Zimbabwe;

o can be easily disseminated, since often more effective local channels of communication are used: pottery technology in Kenya, soybean *daddawa* technology in West Africa, mechanical cassava graters in Nigeria;

o are environmentally sound: cultivation of indigenous crops in Kenya, which can improve soil fertility through nitrogen fixing, and strengthen biodiversity;

o are controlled by the users: the shea butter women described the technical specifications that were needed if the machines were to be of any use to them, as did the users of mechanical cassava graters in Nigeria; women growing soybeans decided how they would be used.

8. Technology policies often create an environment counter-productive

to women's local productive activities by undermining their indigenous knowledge and innovative capacity.

Policy decisions at national, regional or international level can affect women's local food or food-related production, processing and marketing activities. For example, the fuelwood shortage of Kenyan women potters has been made worse by the Lake Basin Development Authority's decision to clear the vegetation to make space for cash crops. Tonga women, having adjusted to the move from the Zambezi River Basin to the less-fertile Binga area, are now threatened by a new proposal to clear the area for cash crop production. Similarly, the promotion of modern dairy plants in Nigeria is diverting scarce milk supplies away from Fulani women.

In addition to disrupting women's local production systems, such policy decisions also have negative environmental consequences. An example of this is the near extinction of the *nkejje* fish and the unrestricted growth of choking algae species in Lake Victoria.

Policies which are made and implemented without regard to local knowledge and practices may even contribute to national disasters by disrupting the harmony between indigenous production systems and their local environments. Policies supporting the cultivation and import of wheat in Sudan at the expense of sorghum, and the cultivation of exotic crops instead of indigenous vegetables have, in various countries, contributed to food security crises. Often, the potential of sorghum and other traditional foods to overcome the worst effects of drought and famine have not yet been fully explored.

Whether the policymakers' lack of recognition of women's local knowledge and production potential is also depriving national economies of potentially lucrative investments still remains to be explored. In Ghana, for example, shea nuts are being exported in the form of whole nuts. Investment in local processing activities would mean that shea butter could be exported in processed form, and the value added would benefit the small producers. In Sierra Leone, women's local salt production currently meets one-fifth of the national demand. The rest is imported with tacit government support. Investments in large-scale solar works proved to be an expensive failure for the country. Support for women's salt-from-silt technology could provide a viable alternative that would decrease the dependency on imports given the foreign currency crisis facing the country. Such policies would need to be designed and implemented in a way that ensured women's continued ownership of their technologies and productive activities.

9. When providing external support to people's technology development, care should be taken so that people do not lose ownership of the initiative.

When technological innovation is undertaken by the local people, the knowledge and skills involved need to be recognized as belonging to the producers themselves. In the few cases where women's indigenous knowledge attracts the attention of scientists, and it is researched and documented by them, women, the source of the information, remain invisible and may lose the ownership of their knowledge and technology. Nutritionists in Uganda initially learned from women about the effectiveness of *nkejje* in the diet: they 'discovered' that it is the high protein content that helps to prevent malnutrition and thus lowers the incidence of measles fatalities. Now the nutrition clinics are running campaigns telling mothers to feed their children with *nkejje*, without acknowledging the fact that women themselves were the origin of this information.

One lesson learned from all the case studies is that while people are capable of responding to change, and developing their own technical solutions, there is still room for the enhancement of local innovative capacity. For external technical support to lead to sustainable development and self-sufficiency, however, it needs to work towards the strengthening of indigenous capacity for technology generation so that information, knowledge and skills remain in the control of the local people.

In the long term outside intervention becomes dispensable. What is needed is not only the participation of the women or men involved, but also their ownership of the initiative.

The case studies in Chapter 3, Section III have shown the different ways that indigenous innovative capacity can be supported by outsiders. In the case of the fuel-efficient stoves in Kenya, a stove technology introduced from outside was based on the technological knowledge and skills of local women potters, and the project was designed around women's identification of their own training needs, working at their own pace. Similarly in the case of livestock production in Peru, a national NGO works alongside women farmers to facilitate the finding of their own solutions to livestock diseases.

In the case of Kenya's indigenous plants, an existing initiative by women was recognized and supported by international and national NGOs, and government extension services for women.

This integrated support has created an enabling environment, wherein the women are able to make the best use of their knowledge and skills. Women have combined traditional techniques with external ones, and improved their production processes.

The collaborative initiative of an international agency with a local NGO in Zaire sets a rare example of how external support can be used to enhance local innovative capacity and leave control firmly in the hands of the women. The project was designed with the long-term objective of proving the efficacy of its approach to extension so that it could be adopted by other programmes. The involvement of a local technology centre as one of the major implementing organizations of the project will be a major channel for its local replication, and it is one step forward in establishing a local mechanism for support to technology development by the people.

5
Guidelines for development practitioners

THE TECHNOLOGY DEVELOPMENT approach promoted throughout this source book is one that fully integrates people's indigenous technical knowledge and supports innovation by the producers and users themselves. The case studies contained in Chapter 3 have illustrated the breadth of people's indigenous knowledge and their capacity to innovate and pointed out the folly of ignoring this in technology development programmes.

For many development practitioners, the mounting evidence of in-depth scientific knowledge among the people they are supposed to be assisting may lead to some questioning of purpose and roles. The purpose of the source book has not been to imply that external assistance is unnecessary and unwanted. Rather, it has aimed at highlighting how development practitioners can and do build on indigenous knowledge and capabilities rather than usurping them. Many of the case studies show how effective it can be for development agencies to link women from different areas with each other so that they transfer and absorb ideas. Others indicate that gender-sensitive scientists and technologists can and do have a role to play in working with rural women to find solutions to problems caused by changing circumstances.

Development practitioners do have a role to play, but it is a new one – one which is based on putting women first and learning from them. This is a very different role from assuming that technologists and extension workers know best and are the mechanism through which 'modern' science and technology are transferred from formal research and development institutions to local people,

from the North to the South. Local producers and technology users are the real 'experts', and scientists and technologists should listen to and build on that knowledge and experience.

The participation of women in technology development should be encouraged not only for the workability of such programmes, but also to empower women to maintain control over resources and decision-making in technical change (McCall, 1987).

Of course, this is all more easily said than done. Many readers, however much they themselves believe in treating women technology users as technical experts, work in organizations which may discourage leaving the initiative in the hands of local people. However, each of us as individuals has a role to play in recognizing and improving the status of women's indigenous knowledge, and contributing to and supporting development programmes which enable the women involved to control the development process.

This final chapter is devoted, therefore, to suggesting guidelines, which will help development practitioners to ask useful questions about women's involvement in technology development, and identify practices and strategies which will support and build on that involvement.

Some guidelines

The fundamental question to ask is: what do women already know and what are they already doing? Everything else follows on from this!

Attitudes

o *Be open:* there is more to learn than to teach. Women have extensive knowledge of their environment, local farming systems, food processing technology, product quality, and marketing. You need to be a good observer, listener and learner to appreciate the wealth of local knowledge.

o *Don't be in a rush:* it takes time to get to know people and to earn their respect and confidence; it takes time even to begin to appreciate what they know; it will take time for women to understand what help is on offer. Gradually work towards an atmosphere of mutual confidence and respect which will facilitate communication.

o *Leave room for women to make their own suggestions:* they are the technical experts.

o *Enable women to decide for themselves about external suggestions:* women should feel comfortable with new ideas, and feel free to accept them with modifications, or reject them. Make sure that suggestions for new techniques, varieties, hardware, organization, etc. fit the particular constraints that women face, such as labour, time, and raw materials. Remember there is always a good reason when women decide not to adopt a technology.

o *Remember that technology is not only a machine:* principles and methods, knowledge and skills, are more important than hardware.

Interaction

o *Talk with women:* discuss priorities and analyse constraints; learn about technical changes and why and how they were made; share information with the women about new techniques and technologies; identify with them what would be useful to their work.

o *Work alongside women:* share routines, and understand roles and responsibilities; learn about production processes, technologies, opportunities and problems by regularly working with women in their homes, fields, and food processing enterprises when possible.

o *Work with groups if appropriate:* women in groups can strengthen and provide support to each other and learn from each other; groups provide a safer environment in which to experiment with different techniques or equipment; even when women prefer to work individually, they may benefit from sharing information in an informal group setting.

Planning

o *Plan with women:* it is their lives that will be affected, so project objectives should reflect their priorities; they should decide activities and risks; they can set targets, monitor progress, and review and learn from success and failure.

o *Let organizations be advised by women:* use local leadership structures if advised to do so; allow natural leaders to emerge.

o *Be flexible:* innovation is often a response to changing circumstances; plans also need to be able to respond to altered conditions, changes of opinion, or lessons learned during the project.

o *Enable women to identify training needs:* they may want help with business skills or marketing rather than technical development; relevant training is vital for sustainability.

Roles

o *Be prepared to act as convener, catalyst, adviser* for local women producers' analysis of problems, and their experimentation with modifications to and changes in production systems through activities such as the following:

- exchange visits with other groups of women: this stimulates women to share skills, ideas and technical experiences, strengthens them as individuals, and may provide valuable marketing or business contacts;
- extension services shaped by women according to their interests: ask women to determine a common theme of their choosing on which to receive extension messages; plan the themes and the timetable for extension visits with the women in advance. Conduct extension visits on a regular basis, with short intervals; provide the inputs on a timely basis. These factors are particularly important in building up confidence in extension advice;
- innovator workshops: these help women to recognize their innovative capacity.

o *Be prepared to act as a go-between:* links between women and local technology consultancy centres are important to building up local capacity.

o *Be prepared to seek out information that women need:* search for and supply local producers with a range of technology choices so they can test and choose on their own; enable them to search for information; find out about useful research and interpret the findings for the women if necessary.

o *Facilitate, support and develop capacity for experimentation:* act as a consultant to transfer not packages and precepts, but principles and methods; reduce risks for women where possible and necessary.

Getting the message across

o *Communicate:* learn local languages and local terms for technical processes, express ideas in a way which people can understand.

o *Use national Research and Development institutions:* teach them about women's technical knowledge and innovative capacities – work with women to make scientists and technologists listen.

o *Enable women's voices to be heard:* arrange meetings where women can speak, facilitate lobbying of local politicians, and support women in applying to donors for funds, assistance or equipment.

These guidelines are partially based on a ICRW Workshop entitled 'Participatory Agriculture Extension Method on a Project with Women Squash Producers in Zaire' at the AWID Conference in November 1991, and the report on the same project prepared by A. Macgowen (1990) (see Appendix II).

Appendix I
Contacts

Below is an organizational contacts list of 'who is doing what' to support grassroots women's indigenous/local technological knowledge and innovation through activities in research, documentation, communication, advocacy, and participatory technology development. This is by no means a complete list, and IT Publications would appreciate receiving information on other organizations and groups working in this area.

African Resource Centre for Indigenous Knowledge (ARCIK)
Nigerian Institute of Social and Economic Research, P.M.B.5, U.I. Post Office, Ibadan, NIGERIA. Tel: +234 22 400501-5; 400550-79; ext's 1551-5; telex: 31119, NISER NG
ARCIK is a resource centre that documents and disseminates information on indigenous knowledge in Africa. The centre is interested in exploring gender in relation to indigenous knowledge and decision-making, indigenous organizations, and indigenous approaches to creativity, innovation and experimentation reflecting local responses to priority problems.

Center for Indigenous Knowledge in Agriculture and Rural Development (CIKARD)
Iowa State University, Ames, Iowa 50011, USA. Tel: +1 515 294 0938
CIKARD is designed to strengthen the capacity of national and international development agencies to improve agricultural production and the quality of life in rural areas, in cost-effective and sustainable ways. CIKARD acts as a clearing house for collecting, documenting and disseminating information on indigenous knowledge on agricultural and rural development; has a newsletter called 'Indigenous Knowledge and Development Monitor'; develops improved methodologies for recording this knowledge; conducts training courses and designs materials on indigenous knowledge for extension and other development workers; and promotes the establishment of regional and national indigenous knowledge centres. Currently CIKARD is conducting research on how gender roles are reflected in indigenous 1) knowledge; 2) decision-making; 3) organizations; 4) problem solving/development.

CIKARD has a network of affiliated indigenous knowledge resource centres at regional and national levels. Regional centres are ARCIK in Nigeria for Africa (see above), and REPPIKA (Regional Program for the Promotion of Indigenous Knowledge in Asia) in the Philippines. The national centres are located in Burkina Faso, Ghana, Kenya, Indonesia, Mexico, Philippines, South Africa, Sri Lanka, and Venezuela. Their contact numbers and addresses can be obtained from CIKARD.

Centre for Rural Health and Social Education (CRHSE)
A-11, Ashok Nagar, Tirupattur 635601, INDIA
The Centre facilitates organization of women's groups for training of women in traditional science and technology practices, such as herbal medicine.

Environment Liaison Centre International (ELCI), Women, Environment, Development Network (WEDNET)
Attention: WEDNET Coordinator, PO Box 72461, Nairobi, KENYA. Tel: +254 562015/562022; fax: +254 562172; e-mail: GN:ELCIDWR
WEDNET is a regional research-based network under the auspices of ELCI. The network carries out multi-disciplinary research with the principal aim of exploring and

documenting women's indigenous knowledge in the management of natural resources in Africa. WEDNET's work highlights the roles of women as key environmental actors as well as custodians of valuable knowledge about local ecosystems.

Fédération des Unions des Groupements Naam (FUGN)
BP 100, Ouahigouya, BURKINA FASO. Tel: +226 550110/550411; fax: +226 550112
FUGN is involved in community development activities in agricultural production, technology development, water and sanitation, income generation, nutrition, education, and environmental conservation with special focus on the role of indigenous knowledge and local production systems.

Fundacion para el Desarallo Agropecuario (FUNDAGRO)
Attention: Ms Susan Poats, Moreno Bellido 127 y Amazonas, PO Box 1716219 CEQ, Quito, ECUADOR. Tel: +593 2 553718/553553/543429/540600; fax: +593 2 503243
FUNDAGRO, a national NGO, is currently involved in formulating a project on sustainable agriculture production and marketing, a major component of which will be to develop a 'Centre for Indigenous Alternative Technology' as a collaborative effort with the President's Office of Indigenous Affairs.

Gender and Local Knowledge Systems in Natural Resource Management Working Sub-group
c/o Futures Group, GENESYS Project, Attention: Constance McCorkle or Alison Meares, 1717 Massachusetts Avenue, NW, Suite 1000, Washington, DC 20036, USA. Tel: +1 202 775-9680; fax: +1 202 775-9699
This working group, organized under Development Strategies for Fragile Lands (DESFIL), a USAID-supported initiative, is a network of development professionals in Washington, DC working in the area of women, development and indigenous knowledge.

Ghana Regional Appropriate Technology Industrial Service (GRATIS)
PO Box 151, Tema, GHANA. Tel: +233 221 4243
GRATIS, a regional NGO involved in the development and dissemination of small-scale and intermediate technologies for grassroots producers, provides urban and rural women with technical support in their productive activities, using participatory methodologies (see case study in Chapter 3, Section III).

Grupo Yanapai
Casilla 264, Huancayo, PERU
Grupo Yanapai is a non-profit research group, consisting of a multi-disciplinary team, promoting participatory research and technology development activities in the peasant agricultural production systems of the Central Sierra of the high Andes (see case study in Chapter 3, Section III).

Information Centre for Low External-Input and Sustainable Agriculture (ILEIA)
Kastanjelaan 5, PO Box 64, 3830 AB Leusden, THE NETHERLANDS. Tel: +31 33 943086; telex: 79380 ETC NL
ILEIA conducts research and documents information on agricultural production systems based on indigenous knowledge, skills and capacity, with the long-term objective that low external-input and sustainable agriculture is:

o widely adopted as a valid approach to agricultural development, complementary to high-external-input agriculture;

o recognized as a means to balance locally available resources and local knowledge
   with modern technologies requiring inputs from elsewhere;
o valued as a useful perspective in planning and implementing agricultural research,
   education and extension;
o developing and consolidating its stock of knowledge and its scientific basis.

Instituto de Estudios Regionales Ayacucho (IERA)
Urb. Maria Parado de Bellido G1-16, Casilla de Correos No: 60, Ayacucho, PERU
IERA has research, documentation, advocacy, dissemination, training, and networking
activities in the area of traditional agriculture and technology, traditional medicine,
health, nutrition, and environment in the Andean Region with specific attention to
women's knowledge, productive and reproductive roles.

*Intermediate Technology Development Group (ITDG), Do It Herself (DIH): Women and
Technological Innovation Programme*
Attention: Helen Appleton, Myson House, Railway Terrace, Rugby CV21 3HT, UK. Tel:
+44 1788 560631; fax: +44 1788 540270
'Do It Herself: Women and Technological Innovation' is a global research and advocacy
programme co-ordinated by ITDG Bangladesh, Peru, Sri Lanka, Sudan, UK and Zimbabwe offices in collaboration with UNIFEM, which aims to document women's local
knowledge and innovations. Recognizing that women's local technical knowledge and
skills have been undervalued, the programme promotes strategies to ensure the equal
access for women as well as men to resources, services and training.

International Center for Research on Women
ICRW, 1717 Massachusetts Avenue, NW, Suite 302, Washington, DC 20036, USA.
Tel: +1 202 797 0007

ICRW, 2a Hampstead Hill Gardens London, NW3 2PL, UK. Tel: +44 171 435 0157
ICRW is a private, non-profit organization dedicated to promoting social and economic
development with women's full participation. Focusing on economic policies, family and
household structure, health and nutrition, and agriculture and the environment, ICRW's
programme consists of policy-oriented research, programme support and analysis services and communications fora. ICRW is the executing agency for a participatory technology development project with women in Zaire (see case study in Chapter 3, Section III).

The International Centre of Insect Physiology and Ecology (ICIPE)
PO Box 30772, Nairobi, Kenya. Tel: + 254 2 802501/3/9; fax: +254 2 803360
ICIPE is primarily involved in conducting research in integrated control methodologies
for crop and livestock pests and also strengthening of scientific and technological capacities of countries of the South in insect science and its application through training and
collaborative work. Within the context of its mandate to develop appropriate technologies
for the rural low-income farming households, ICIPE recognizes and actively seeks to
integrate women farmers' informal knowledge, practices and skills into its programmes.

International Federation of Inventors Association (IFIA)
Attention: Farag Moussa, 3 rue Bellot, 1206 Geneva, SWITZERLAND. Tel: +41 22
346-5379; fax: +41 22 789-3076
IFIA, an international network of inventors associations around the world, promotes
the recognition of women inventors past and present and assists in the formation of
women inventors associations.

International Institute for Environment and Development (IIED)
3 Endsleigh Street, London WC1H 0DD, UK. Tel: +44 171 388 2117
IIED is currently compiling an annotated bibliography on the role of wild foods in sustainable livelihoods under its Sustainable Agriculture Programme. The aim of the bibliography is to produce a readable commentary, drawing on both published and unpublished research, on the importance of wild foods (forest fruits, insects, grasses, 'weeds', etc.) for both agricultural and pastoral peoples throughout the tropics. The review will also help in the identification of research gaps to provide a foundation for further case studies, with the ultimate goal of presenting policy recommendations on the use of wild resources for agricultural research and development planning. Contact people for this programme are: Mary Melnyk, Centre for Environmental Technology, Imperial College, 48 Prince's Gardens, London SW7 2PE, UK. Tel: +44 171 5985111; or Jules Petty or Ian Scoones of IIED (address as above).

International Women's Tribune Centre (IWTC)
777 UN Plaza, New York, NY 10017, USA. Tel: +1 212 687 8633; fax: +1 212 661 2704; Cable: Tribcen
IWTC is an information and communication support group for women's and community organizations in Africa, Asia, Latin America, Western Asia, the Caribbean and the South Pacific. Its quarterly newsletter, *The Tribune*, and other action-oriented publications offer strategies for action and resources in four main programme areas: information and communication, science and technology, women organizing (empowerment/ leadership) and community economic development. IWTC also offers technical assistance and training in the production of information materials. Science and technology is a major programme area, with emphasis on demystifying and popularizing science and technology.

Ix Chel Tropical Research Foundation
Ix Chel Farm, San Ignacio Cayo, BELIZE, Central America. Tel: +501 092 3310; fax: +501 092 2057
Ix Chel is involved in the collection and recording of indigenous medicinal plant knowledge and traditional methods for health and natural resource maintenance. The Foundation holds traditional healers' conferences to share information on wild medicinal plants cultivation and preparation. The foundation works with Belize Traditional Healers Association and Belize Rural Women's Association in providing support to traditional healers and to formulate training and education programmes on medicinal plant use, and primary health care appropriate for village life. The organization uses both Spanish and English.

Kenya Energy and Environment Organisation (KENGO)
Natural Resources Research and Development Programme, PO Box 48197, Nairobi, KENYA. Tel: +254 748281/74947; fax: +254 749382
KENGO, which is a coalition of grassroots women's groups involved in research and community development activities using appropriate technologies and locally available resources, has a programme supporting women's production of indigenous food crops and the production of indigenous vegetables. The programme includes information dissemination on indigenous food crops, and encourages women's adaptation of new technologies such as bio-intensive gardening and modification of indigenous technologies (see case study in Chapter 3, Section III).

Marga Institute
61 Isipathana Mawatha, PO Box 601, Colombo 5, SRI LANKA. Tel: +94 1 585186/581514; fax: +94 1 580-585
The Institute, which is engaged in development studies and research and has a women's studies division, has a research and publication project on women as initiators of and responders to change in agricultural technology.

Servicios Multiples de Technologias Apropiadas (SEMTA)
Casilla 15401, La Paz, BOLIVIA. Tel: +591 2 360042; fax: +591 2 391458
SEMTA, a national NGO, is involved in technology development and dissemination with rural women using participatory methodologies with specific attention to women's indigenous technologies, local agricultural and ecological systems. South-South technology transfer, women's ownership of technology development initiatives, and support to women's own innovations constitute the main focus of SEMTA's work. Agriculture and energy are the main sectors of SEMTA activities with women.

Tanzania Women's Media Association (TAMWA)
Umati Building, 1st Floor, PO Box 6143, Dar es Salaam, TANZANIA. Tel: +255 51 23784/32181; fax: + 255 51 31709
TAMWA is a non-profit organization whose mandate is to capture the voices of women who have not been heard, and support rural women by promoting their concerns through conventional media as well as through more traditional communication forms such as visual, theatre, folk and artistic media. TAMWA is currently involved in a project for gathering and documenting information on women's indigenous knowledge of medicinal plants and cosmetics. TAMWA's quarterly publication 'Sauti Ya Siti', a Tanzania women's magazine which serves as a forum of discussion and communication for women, is available in Swahili and English.

Veld Products Research
Attention: Mr Frank Taylor, PO Box 2020, Gabarone, BOTSWANA
Veld Products Research is an NGO research organization focusing on assisting rural communities in managing and marketing their indigenous resources on a sustainable basis.

World Neighbors
5116 North Portland Avenue, Oklahoma City, OK 73112, USA. Tel: +1 405 946-3333; toll free (US only): 1-800-242-6387; telex: 510 600-2674; fax: +1 405 946-9994
WN, an international development organization working with local communities in Asia, Africa and Latin America, develops communications and educational materials which reflect the focus on participatory methodologies and encourage the self-sufficiency of people in rural communities throughout the world. These materials are available from World Neighbors.

UN agencies

United Nations Children's Educational Fund (UNICEF)
3 United Nations Plaza, New York, NY 10017, USA. Tel: +1 212 326-7000; fax: +1 212 888-7454; telex: 175989

UNICEF's work in the area of indigenous knowledge includes the following: funding of a meeting of 'shamans' and traditional doctors in Iquitos, Peru (August 1991) to promote health education and sanitation, on the basis of which a bilingual intercultural program is being implemented; and conduct of knowledge, attitude and practice surveys in Central America, namely Guatemala, Costa Rica, and Panama, to serve as the basis of support activities in education, health, water supply and sanitation.

United Nations Development Fund for Women (UNIFEM)
304 East 45th Street, 6th Floor, New York, NY 10017, USA. Tel: +1 212 906-6400; fax: + 1 212 906-6705
Grassroots women's local knowledge and skills constitute a major component of UNIFEM's agricultural programmes in Asia and the Pacific, Africa, Latin America and the Caribbean, as well as its global science and technology strategy. Recognizing the importance and value of women's grassroots knowledge and skills, the agency funds programmes which promote active participation of women in development programmes and policies.

United Nations Development Programme (UNDP) Regional Bureau for Latin America and the Caribbean, Global Environment Facility
1 UN Plaza, 22nd Floor, New York, NY 10017, USA. Tel: +1 212 906-5468; fax: +1 212 906-5892
UNDP has three projects in Bolivia, Ecuador and Colombia, which aim to explore and utilize local knowledge and traditions to develop viable means for managing natural resources in the indigenous communities of the Amazon Basin. The agency also has small grants of $1000 to $20 000 to intermediary organizations and NGOs for indigenous people's activities.

United Nations Transnational Corporations and Management Division (UNTCMD), Department of Social and Economic Development
Lorraine Ruffing, Working Group on Indigenous Populations, Room DC2-1318, 2 UN Plaza, New York, NY 10017, USA. Tel: +1 212 963 3154; fax: +1 212 963-3062/2146
UNTCMD is currently undertaking a research and database project on the activities of transnational corporations on indigenous lands. A questionnaire, which included specific sections on indigenous productive activities, methods/techniques, subsistence systems, and disruptions caused by external interventions, was sent to 750 indigenous groups in Latin America and 340 groups in Africa and Asia. These groups now form part of an electronic network which can be used for a variety of purposes.

Appendix II
References

Abeywardane, P. (1990) *Jak and Bread Fruit Preservation in Sri Lanka*, Colombo, Sri Lanka. Research paper presented at the ITDG Seminar 'Do It Herself: Women and Technological Innovation in Asia' in Dhaka, Bangladesh.

Adjebeng-Asem, S. (1990) 'The Nigerian Cassava Grater' in Gamser, Appleton, Carter (eds), *Tinker, Tiller, Technical Change*. IT Publications, London, UK.

Ahmed, I. (1985) *Technology and Rural Women*, Allen & Unwin, London.

Appleton, H. and Ilkkaracan, I. (forthcoming) *The Technological Capabilities of Women and Girls in Developing Countries*. Chapter in 'Innovations in Science and Technology', UNESCO.

Awa, N.E. (1989) 'Underutilization of Women's Indigenous Knowledge in Agricultural and Rural Development Programmes: The effect of stereotypes' in Warren *et al.*

Azhaira, J. and Dirar, H. (1979) 'Studies on Natural Water Coagulants in the Sudan', Khartoum, Sudan in *Water SA*, Vol. 5, No. 2.

Carr, M. (1984) *Blacksmith, Baker, Roofing Sheet Maker*, IT Publications, London, UK.

Chambers, R., Pacey, A., Thump, L. (eds) (1989) *Farmer First: Farmer innovations and agricultural research*, IT Publications, London, UK.

Compton, J.L. (1989) 'Strategies and Methods for the Access, Integration and Utilization of Indigenous Knowledge in Agriculture and Rural Development' in Warren *et al.*

Cowley, G. (1989) 'The Electronic Goddess: Computerizing Bali's ancient irrigation rites', *Newsweek*, 6 March: 50.

Dey, J. (1981) *Irrigated Rice Development Projects and the Farming System in the Gambia*, Banjul, Gambia.

Dirar, H. (1991) *Processing of Traditional Fermented Sorghum Foods and Drinks of the Sudan*, Khartoum, Sudan. Research paper presented at the ITDG/UNIFEM seminar 'Do It Herself: Women and Technological Innovation in Africa' in Harare, Zimbabwe.

Fernandez, M. (1988) 'Towards a Participatory Systems Approach', *ILEIA Newletter*, 1988, Vol. 4, No. 3, Leusden, The Netherlands.

Fernandez, M. *Participatory Action Research and the Farming Systems Approach with Highland Peasants* SR-CRSP Technical Report No. 75, Columbia MO, University of Missouri, Department of Rural Sociology.

Fleuret, P. (1985) 'The Social Organization of Water Control in the Tatia Hills, Kenya', *American Ethnologist* 12(1): 103–118.

Gill, D.S. (1987) *Effectiveness of Agricultural Extension Services in Reaching Rural Women: A synthesis of studies from five African countries*. Paper presented at FAO Workshop on 'Improving the Effectiveness of Agricultural Extension Services in Reaching Rural Women' in Harare, Zimbabwe.

Gubbels and Iddi, A. (undated) *Cultivation and Utilisation of Soybeans among West African Women through Family Health Animation Efforts*, World Neighbors Case Study, Oklahoma, USA.

ICRW Workshop (1991) *Participatory Agriculture Extension Method on a Project with Women Squash Producers in Zaire*, organized by Catherine Reid at AWID Conference, 21–24 November.

ILEIA (1988) 'Participative Technology Development', *ILEIA Newsletter* Vol. 4, No. 3, Leusden, The Netherlands.

Jahn, S. and Dirar, H. (1979) 'Studies on Natural Water Coagulants in the Sudan with special reference to *Moringa oleifera* seeds'. *Water SA* Vol. 5, No. 2.

Katumba, R. (1991) *Knowledge and Development*, IDRC Reports, April.

Lahai, B. (1991) *Salt Extraction in Sierra Leone*. Research paper presented at the ITDG/UNIFEM seminar 'Do It Herself: Women and Technological Innovation in Africa' in Harare, Zimbabwe.

Lansing, S. (1987) 'Balinese Water Temples and the Management of Irrigation', *American Anthropologist* 89(2): 326–341.

Macgowen, A. (1990) *EPIC/CAL Mid-term Assessment*, prepared by ICRW for USAID Area Food and Marketing Development Project, Kinshasa, Zaire.

Massaquoi, J.G.M. (1990) 'Salt from Silt in Sierra Leone', in Gamser, Appleton, Carter (eds), *Tinker, Tiller, Technical Change*, IT Publications, London, UK.

Maybury, R.H. (1982) *Financing of Research, Invention and Innovation*, Science and Technology Unit, The World Bank, Washington, DC.

McCall, M. (1987) *Indigenous Knowledge Systems as the Basis for Participation: East African potentials*, Working Paper No. 36, University of Twente, Technology and Development Group, Enschede.

McCorkle, C. (1987) 'Price, Preference and Practice: Farmers' grain disposal decisions in a Burkibane community' in *The Dynamics of Grain Marketing in Burkina Faso*, Vol. III, Ann Arbor, MI and Ouagadougou; University of Michigan for Center for Research on Economic Development.

McCorkle, C. (1989) *Management of Animal Health and Disease in an Indigenous Andean Community*, SR-CRSP Publication No. 5, Columbia MO, University of Missouri, Department of Rural Sociology.

McCorkle with M.F. Nolan, K. Jamtgaard, J.L. Gills (1989) *Social Research in Agricultural R&D: Lessons from the Small Ruminant CRSP*. Agriculture and Human Values, 6(3): pg. 42–51 (in draft form).

Mehratu, S. and Hahn, N. (1986) *Daddawa*. Paper presented at the Seminar on Nigerian Food Culture, Institute of African Studies, University of Ibadan.

Moussa, F. (1991) *Women Inventors Honoured by the World Intellectual Property Organisation*, Geneva.

Mpofu, N. and Mpande, R. (1991) *Innovation Among the Tonga Women in Zimbabwe*, Harare, Zimbabwe. Research paper presented at the ITDG/UNIFEM seminar 'Do It Herself: Women and Technological Innovation in Africa' in Harare, Zimbabwe.

Mutagaywa, J. (1991) *Women Potters in Western Kenya*, Kisumu, Kenya. Research paper presented at the ITDG/UNIFEM seminar 'Do It Herself: Women and Technological Innovation in Africa' in Harare, Zimbabwe.

Ogana, W. (1988) 'Harvesting Milk for Tomorrow' in *All Africa Press Service*, Science and Technology Features Service, Nairobi, Kenya.

Ogana, W. (1991) *Indigenous Vegetables in Kenya*, Nairobi, Kenya. Research paper presented at the ITDG/UNIFEM seminar 'Do It Herself: Women and Technological Innovation in Africa in Harare, Zimbabwe.

Ogana, W. (undated) 'Where Women Profit from Crops Grown by Womenfolk' in *The Herald*, Harare, Zimbabwe.

Ogana, W. (undated) 'In Kenya, Modern Agriculture May Worsen Drought's Effects,' in *All Africa Press Service*, Science and Technology Features Service, Nairobi, Kenya.

Ogana, W. (undated) *Food Preservation*, Nairobi, Kenya.

Onabolu, A.O. (1988) *Cassava Products: UNICEF/IITA program on household food security and nutrition*, International Institute of Tropical Agriculture (IITA), Ibadan, Nigeria.